GPO staff in 1916
Business as Usual

STEPHEN FERGUSON

MERCIER PRESS
IRISH PUBLISHER - IRISH STORY

MERCIER PRESS

Cork

www.mercierpress.ie

© Stephen Ferguson, 2005; revised, enlarged edition, 2012

ISBN: 978 1 85635 994 8

10 9 8 7 6 5 4 3 2 1

A CIP record for this title is available from the British Library

Printed and bound in the EU.

GPO staff in 1916
Business as Usual

The ruined GPO seen from Nelson's Pillar.

(Courtesy of the BMPA)

CONTENTS

Acknowledgements

This book is a revised and more extensive edition of one I wrote a few years ago as '*Self respect and a little extra leave*' – *G.P.O. Staff in 1916*. I would like to thank the British Postal Museum and Archive (BPMA, images © Royal Mail Group Ltd 2012) in London, the National Library of Ireland and An Post for permission to reproduce material in their care. The editorial advice of Dr L. K. Ferguson and Dr K. P. Ferguson is much appreciated, as is the assistance of a number of colleagues, current and retired, within An Post.

The ruins of Dublin's city centre.

(An Post archives)

Introduction

Much has been written about the 1916 Rising over the years and the GPO, as the headquarters of the Rising, has been assured a unique place in Irish history. Surely no other postal headquarters can have witnessed the proclamation of a Republic in similar circumstances and this distinction has drawn into the GPO many visitors whose interest in the Post Office would otherwise be limited to buying a stamp or paying a bill.

The memoirs and reminiscences of those who took part in the Rising have helped to shed light on the events of Easter week, but they have sometimes also highlighted inconsistencies and inaccuracies in the accounts which can make it difficult to know exactly what happened. This will always be the case, but the great secrecy in which the Rising was planned, the confusion which followed the last minute cancellation of 'manoeuvres' and the swift execution of the principal leaders are factors which have accentuated the difficulties in understanding the events of Easter week.

The records housed in the British Postal Museum and Archive in London are unusually interesting because of the detail and freshness of the factual information which they provide on the progress of the rebellion. Here, in the official reports of various Dublin and provincial GPO staff, lies not merely an exciting account of Post Office people in turbulent times, but also nuggets of new information that should be of interest both to academic historians of the Rising and to the many people for whom the drama of 1916 holds a special fascination. Confidential police reports held in the United Kingdom National Archives provide extensive details of surveillance on some of the Post Office people who were secretly planning to cripple the Irish communications network at the outbreak of the rebellion. Some thirty-five years after the Rising, a few of those men gave statements to the Bureau of Military History which described from the inside what the G-men could only observe from the outside.

What is also of importance is the unique perspective that Post Office papers provide on the Rising. Composed at the time or within a couple of days of the suppression of the Rising, the Post Office memoranda are high-quality, contemporary eyewitness accounts of events almost as they happen. Such was the scope and breadth of Post Office operations at the time that accounts of the rebellion from several locations throughout the city – the GPO, the Crown Alley Telephone Exchange, Aldborough House, Dublin Castle and Amiens Street station – are available to the historian. In the comments and private memoir, *Irish Experiences in War*, of A. H. Norway, the Post Office Secretary, there is the discernment of a high-ranking official who, though emphatically a civil servant and not a politician, was in an excellent position to assess sentiment before the Rising and to appreciate government reaction in its wake. No other institution is able to provide such a rich, composite insight into the events of Easter week 1916. Reaction to events in Dublin, as seen through the eyes of other patriotic Irishmen in France, is to be found in the wonderful collection of trench letters posted to Monica Roberts from the Front.

Through many accounts and different viewpoints, the Post Office offers perspectives on the Rising that are unique in their immediacy, their freshness and their freedom from historical interpretation. What is of particular interest, however, for today's GPO staff is the picture that emerges of a Post Office that is so resolutely committed to maintaining and restoring its service. It is an intriguing story of how ordinary men and women react in extraordinary circumstances – motivated, in Norway's view, out of no more than simple 'self-respect' and the prospect of 'a little extra leave'.

Sketch map showing the location of GPO staff during and immediately after the Rising.

(Stephen Ferguson)

Dublin's GPO – Communications Hub and Fortress

There is surely no other building in Ireland that can draw from Irish people the same recognition, affection and respect that is felt for Dublin's General Post Office. For nearly two hundred years now, it has stood in the capital's O'Connell Street, an ever-present and impartial witness to the dramas, great and small, that unfold before it day by day. It is important not just as the long-standing principal office of the Irish Post Office and as a building of considerable architectural significance in Dublin's city centre, but also as the birthplace, in Easter 1916, of an independent Ireland. No other Irish public building can claim this unique heritage and, before hearing the voices of the GPO staff who in 1916 knew the building only as the headquarters of the Post Office, it is fitting that the grand old lady of O'Connell Street should set the scene for the events that would change the course of Irish history.

The old GPO had been located in College Green but by the start of the nineteenth century was in poor repair, so when a site which had been the location of a temporary military barracks became available in what was then Sackville Street, the idea of building a grand new Post Office as the centrepiece of a streetscape that would run all the way from the Liffey to the Rotunda, was accepted. The architect selected was Francis Johnston, a County Armagh man, who was architect to the Board of Works. The son of a builder who also dabbled in architecture, Johnston was born in 1760 and started his career as architect to the Archbishop of Armagh, Richard Robinson. He did work, both ecclesiastical and domestic, for a number of patrons before his appointment in 1805 to the Board of Works where the emphasis was on civic architecture.

The foundation stone of the new GPO was laid on 12 August 1814 and the building was opened for business less than four years later on 6 January 1818. It is, by any standards, a very fine Post Office and predates – much to the satisfaction of Irish Post Office pride – the completion of a new London GPO by over a decade. It is, in keeping with much of Johnston's work, a solid and rather severe building, a touch institutional perhaps, in the opinion of the late Maurice Craig, who did so much to foster an appreciation of Dublin's architecture. Built of Wicklow granite with a portico of Portland stone, the building was just over 220 feet long, 150 deep and rose 50 feet to the top of the cornice. Six Ionic columns support the central portico which spans the pavement in front of the building and, from their commanding position above the pediment, three fine symbolic statues by John Smyth survey the street. Hibernia, with her harp, stands proudly in the centre with Fidelity, the cardinal virtue of any postal service, on her left and Mercury, the winged messenger of the gods, on her right.

As GPO business developed and expanded during the nineteenth century, space became tight and the building was subject to various additions and refurbishments. Long before Pearse and Connolly entered the building on Easter Monday 1916, business expansion into areas like savings, telegraphs and telephones meant that staff accommodation in the GPO had disappeared. By the beginning of the twentieth century the building had been internally remodelled so many times that Francis Johnston himself might have found it hard to recognise his own work. The main Public Office was quite inadequate for business and the building was the butt of Dublin wits who said it was the only building on the street which had no door – the main public entrance being around the corner in Prince's Street!

Dublin's General Post Office – a building of remarkable emotional and historical interest.

(Stephen Ferguson)

The Board of Works undertook a programme of significant renovation, including the acquisition of neighbouring property, in stages, in the decade leading up to the Rising. The railings outside the GPO were removed, the main entrance doorway was restored to the front of the building and long-standing critics of the cramped and dingy Public Office were silenced by the creation of a spacious, light-filled public area, fitted out with Burmese teak counters and vitreous mosaic floors. A beautiful public telephone kiosk, crowned by a clock – destined to be the detention place of one of the first prisoners of the forthcoming Irish Republic – can be clearly seen in the photograph of the interior taken on completion of the building works in March 1916. The press, the public and the editor of *The Irish Builder* were uniformly impressed: little did they know that the time to appreciate this gleaming new office would be limited to just a few weeks.

What, it may be asked, was in the minds of the 1916 leaders as they watched progress on the GPO building work? Tom Clarke's shop was only round the corner and James Connolly's Liberty Hall a short stroll down Abbey Street. They must have seen it virtually every day and been into it dozens of times. When was it decided that the GPO would serve as headquarters of the rebellion? Who took that decision? Such was the secrecy that attended the planning of the Rising – secrecy ensuring that, on this occasion at least, agents and informers were not able to penetrate the core of the movement – that with the execution of its leaders it became impossible to answer these questions.

The building, certainly, had defensive strengths, with Johnston's central block possessing an 'opulent severity', something that sounds like it would at least discourage potential besiegers.[1] Its thick walls, basement vaults and extensive size suggest a structure that could well serve as a temporary fortress. Its roofline commanded a strategic sweep of the city centre and would have made an assault difficult and costly. It occupied a large site, with good communication lines to the north and west, although with a less satisfactory route to the south, down Williams' Lane. If symbolism is needed, it could be said that the GPO was the civil representative of imperial power on the north side of the Liffey, the building which most prominently flew the flag on the occasion of royal visits.

What can be said with certainty is that someone within the inner circle that planned the Rising appreciated the importance of communications. Martin King, for instance, a cable joiner in the Post Office and Irish Citizen Army man, recalled being asked by James Connolly towards the end of 1915 'if he wanted

1   Maurice Craig, *Dublin 1660–1860*, p. 285.

to cut communication with England, how would he go about it.'[2] That there was also a perceptive understanding of broader public relations issues is clear from the composition and printing of the Proclamation, from the publication of *Irish War News* and from the ingenious attempt to broadcast by Morse code news of the Rising from the roof of a premises across the road from the GPO. The last generation of revolutionaries sought control of radio and television stations, today's have at their disposal the extraordinary power of the internet, a medium much less amenable to the exclusive control of a single authority. Those who planned the Rising were not so well equipped, but clearly understood the relevance and importance of the well-established telegraph network and the newer telephone system.

On Easter Monday 1916, confusion from the previous day's countermanding orders, lack of men and perhaps a little bad luck destroyed what had been a bold plan. Within a short time, the ingenuity and bravery of Post Office staff wrested back control of communications and, for all practical purposes, determined the outcome of the Rising. This is why the Post Office mattered and why, above all else, the GPO became the headquarters of the 1916 leaders.

---

2   Bureau of Military History (BMH) WS 0543.

A. H. Norway – Secretary of the Irish Post Office

Arthur Hamilton Norway, Secretary of the Irish Post Office during the 1916 Rising, occupies a place of particular importance in the history of the rebellion, a place which has, however, been obscured, perhaps by the fact that he was merely an English civil servant who happened to find himself at the head of the greatest Department and largest employer in Ireland during a period of unparalleled turbulence in Dublin.[1] His appointment to Ireland at the time of the Home Rule debates, his knowledge of affairs in the run-up to 1916 and the personal responsibility he shouldered during and in the immediate aftermath of the Rising itself mark him out as an observer of unusual perception. His accommodation in the old Royal Hibernian Hotel in Dawson Street – a minute's walk from Countess Markievicz's position in the College of Surgeons, another to the defensive fortress that was Trinity College and just a short stroll from the GPO or Thomas MacDonagh in Jacob's Biscuit Factory – placed him at the very heart of the Rising in Dublin and for that week his room became the headquarters of the Post Office in Ireland. From there, seated by the telephone and assisted by his wife, who published an account of the rebellion that is not only readable and vivid but also very fair, he and the few staff who could get to him coolly endeavoured to restore communications and bring order to chaos, while his formal reports to Sir Evelyn Murray, the Post Office Secretary in London, concentrated on Post Office business rather

---

1   At this time the Post Office was a government department, just like the Inland Revenue, the Admiralty and so on.

A. H. Norway, Secretary to the
Post Office in Ireland.
(Courtesy of the BMPA)

than the general destruction taking place around him and the
personal dangers under which his staff were working. His undated
memoir, *Irish Experiences in War*, written about ten years after the
Rising when he was retired, recalls in tranquillity the emotion and
turmoil of that week and the circumstances which brought it to
pass.[2] Since it was composed for private circulation only, he felt
free to express there opinions, still inevitably clothed in a degree of
diplomatic reserve, which he could not voice in anything designed
for publication.

The man who casually dropped into his office in the GPO on
Easter Monday 1916, en route to lunch with his wife and son,

2   A copy of this is in the National Library (MS 24,894) amongst the
papers of Dr León Ó Broin who, like Norway, became Secretary of the
Post Office. It is published in Keith Jeffery's *The Sinn Féin Rebellion as
They Saw It*.

was born in 1859 and entered the civil service as a clerk in the Inland Revenue Department in 1880. He was transferred to the Post Office in 1883 and spent his early career there in the foreign and colonial branch of the Secretary's office where he gained a reputation as a promising and highly efficient young man. He rose through the ranks within the Secretary's office and was appointed Assistant Secretary in 1907. When the secretaryship in Ireland fell vacant in 1912, Norway applied for the job and got it. It was a lateral move for him and by no means an obvious career decision but, after nearly thirty years in broadly the same occupation, he may have wanted a new challenge and a change of scene suited his personal circumstances as both his wife and elder son were recovering from periods of ill health. The top job in the Irish Post Office required a particular political sensitivity as well as managerial competence and Norway, who was broadly sympathetic to the Home Rule proposals then under discussion, was seen as a safe appointment.

In Ireland the appointment was criticised by some as the imposition of yet another Englishman over the heads of deserving Irishmen, but Norway's tact, even-handedness and willingness to listen – in the most testing of circumstances – had won him considerable respect and a reputation for fairness by the time he returned to London as Assistant Secretary in 1917. Progressive deafness may, by this stage, have impaired his chances of promotion to the top couple of positions in the Post Office, but his service was recognised by the award of a CB (Companion of the Most Honourable Order of the Bath) in the New Year's Honours list of 1918. He retired in 1920 and died in 1938.

Son of a woman who wrote several children's stories and father of the popular novelist, Nevil Shute, Norway was himself an author of broad taste. As a young civil servant he helped an older lady, Charlotte Riddell, with the production of *The Government Official*, a collaboration which he no doubt put behind him as soon as possible following a review which said, 'We never met a duller group than the characters in *The Government Official*' where 'the sordid lives of commonplace people are traced with exasperating care'. *Parson Peter, a Tale of the Dart* came out under his own name and a few travel books, especially the *Highways and Byways* volume on Devon and Cornwall, illustrated by the popular Coleraine-born artist Hugh Thompson, were well received. A Cornish ancestor may have been the inspiration for his *History of the Post-Office Packet Service* which concentrated on the Falmouth packet station. It is a well-written narrative of the days when Post Office ships often had to fight to make port, but he has little to say about the Irish routes such as the Dublin–Holyhead mail boat which 'confronted no dangers worth speaking of' – written, of course, long before the First World War – and the Donaghadee–Portpatrick route which was 'still less interesting'.[3] His appointment to the Irish job – certainly once the Great War began – may well have caused him to reconsider this rather peremptory dismissal of the dangers of the Irish Sea crossing.

Norway rented a large house, Southhill, on Mount Merrion Avenue in Blackrock not too far from the house built by John Lees, one of his predecessors in the position of Secretary of the Irish Post Office. The house provided convenient access to the city centre and the GPO, whilst offering plenty of space and gardens for his family. His granddaughter expressed what she thought the move to Ireland meant for Norway and his family:

> In London there had been several men of the calibre of my grandfather who were in the Post Office, and all doing pretty much the same work,

3   *History of the Post-Office Packet Service*, p. 14.

but in Ireland my grandfather was the big frog in the small puddle. They had a mansion to keep up and they were known in the area, and so they had to live a little bit more constrained a life perhaps, because they were in the public eye. They had a position to keep up.[4]

In his autobiography, *Slide Rule*, Nevil Shute recalls the house and its surroundings in Blackrock which, for his elder brother Fred and himself who were used to more cramped London quarters, 'opened up new country pleasures we had hardly dreamed of'.[5] Fred entered Trinity College and Nevil, who was boarding at Shrewsbury, spent his holidays in Dublin. For Norway, after the initial period of adjustment and acclimatisation to the fact that he was now immediately responsible for a staff of some 17,000 people and operation of the Department's entire service throughout Ireland, the move must have seemed a wise one. He set himself to his work with vigour, devoting particular energy to the remodelling of the GPO's public office, a 'miserable, dirty little place that would have been a disgrace to a small country town' and the reinstitution, in line with Francis Johnston's original design, of the main entrance under the central portico.[6] The end result, opened to the public just six weeks before it was to be utterly destroyed, represented a wonderful transformation and Norway must have taken justifiable pride in the completion of the project. His wife, certainly, was proud of his achievement and, writing to her sister shortly after the Rising, recalled the interior of the public office:

4   Heather Mayfield, interviewed in 1999 (Nevil Shute Norway Foundation).
5   Nevil Shute, *Slide Rule*, p. 14.
6   Mrs Hamilton Norway, *The Sinn Fein Rebellion as I saw it*, p. 70. Her record of Easter week, published as a series of letters in July 1916, is a vivid and perceptive account of events as they unfold.

The roof was a large glass dome, with elaborate plaster work, beautiful white pillars, mosaic floor, counters all of red teak wood and bright brass fittings everywhere – a public building of which any great city might be proud.[7]

By the time the war broke out in August 1914, Norway would have been well-known in the upper echelons of Dublin society and his wife, 'very well up in all the usages of polite society', must have settled comfortably into the graceful rounds of pre-1916 Irish life.[8] When Sir Mathew Nathan, a well-travelled colonial administrator and Norway's old boss in the Post Office, was appointed Irish Under Secretary in 1914, Norway could confidently offer him advice on the political conclusions which would be drawn from his membership of various Dublin clubs.

The war soon undermined what must have been a pleasant, if slightly provincial, existence and a year later personal tragedy had shattered what serenity remained. Fred Norway interrupted his studies at Trinity to join the army. In June 1915 he was wounded not far from Armentières and died from his wounds three weeks later. He was only nineteen. Heather Mayfield recounted the circumstances in her interview over eighty years afterwards:

He was wounded after he'd only been in the war for a few months, and … while they were not serious, there were no antibiotics then, and he did not survive the wounds. He died a rather lingering death, but it's interesting to know that one of the Army officers over Fred had contacted my grandparents and said, 'Look Fred has had these rather nasty wounds. Perhaps you could come along and be with him', and

7   *Ibid.*, p. 71.
8   *Slide Rule*, p. 14.

such was the nature of war in those times that my grandparents went along and were with Fred, behind the lines, when he died.

His sword, his commission and a few treasured mementoes were in Norway's safe in the GPO when the building was occupied on Easter Monday. Fred's death affected the family deeply and the house in Mount Merrion became for them a constant reminder of former, happier times. Norway gave up the lease and took temporary rooms instead in the city centre and so it happened that, for a brief spell at Easter 1916, the Royal Hibernian Hotel – an establishment connected in previous generations with the Post Office through the famous coach proprietor, Charles Bianconi – became Dublin's *de facto* GPO.

CHARLES · WILLIAM · CHESTER · MYLES
ARTHUR · HILL · NEALE
JAMES · EDWARD · THORNHILL · NELIS
THOMAS · VILLIERS · T · THACKER · NEVILLE
HARRY · LONSDALE · NORTH
FREDERICK · HAMILTON · NORWAY
CLAUD · ROBERT · BARTON · NOYES
WILLIAM · ALBERT · NEVILLE · OAKSHOTT
MAURICE · JAMES · O'CONNELL
HUBERT · MICHAEL · O'CONNOR
WILLIAM · MOYLE · O'CONNOR

The war memorial in Trinity College Dublin. Norway's son, Fred, who died from his wounds in 1915, is named.

(Stephen Ferguson)

HEAD OR HARP –
POLITICS IN THE POST

The Post Office did not start life as a great public utility, but as an instrument of government designed to sift the currents of political activity. Wolfe Tone, for instance, often refers to the dangers of committing anything secret to the mail and, even when he was in France, his fear of government spies and French informers remained. However, by the time Norway took up office in Ireland, the Post Office had become a great commercial organisation where there was little need to intercept and open letters. The power to do so remained, of course, and as Irish cultural identity reasserted itself in the opening years of the twentieth century and the Home Rule debates generated political tension, the Post Office in Ireland once again played a minor role in the larger political drama.

Activities which were entirely innocent in origin, such as the renewed interest in Irish as a means of daily communication, might be subverted for political ends. It was alleged by some, for instance, that the secretary of the Gaelic League 'had appealed to members to address their letters in Irish to annoy the Post Office'.[1] The matter gave rise to correspondence between Irish language enthusiasts and Post Office officials, who felt that the efficiency of postal operations was being jeopardised by a practice calculated to have a political effect. The choice of some nationalist correspondents to affix the stamp, which bore the King's head, upside down on their letters certainly was a political decision.

Further difficulty arose when Sinn Féin, in an effort to raise funds and promote awareness of the organisation, printed small

---

1   See R. B. D. French in *Hermathena,* No. CII, 1966.

This envelope addressed to Thomas Clarke, signatory of the Proclamation, bears a Sinn Féin propaganda label beside the usual stamp.

(An Post archives)

labels to be sold and stuck on envelopes going through the post. Designs, based on Irish history and culture, were probably drawn by Lily Williams, a friend of the Sinn Féin President, Arthur Griffith, whose background in printing gave him an appreciation of the power of graphic and visual propaganda. They were sold at 2/6 a gross and they were, as Griffith explained in the *Sinn Féin* newspaper, 'intended to be affixed to all correspondence of Sinn Féiners as a visible sign that this is Ireland.'[2] Finnish nationalists had undertaken a similar project when they sought to draw attention to the fact that Finland was not a province of Russia but 'a nation … defending its liberties against foreign despotism.'

There was never any intention to defraud the Post Office, but their use did give rise to delays in handling the mail and from 1 August 1908 the Post Office decided that any letters bearing private labels on the address side would be returned to the sender. Labels of both unionist and nationalist hue, however, were produced from time to time in subsequent years and the souvenir

2   *Sinn Féin* weekly, 4 January 1908.

publications which followed the end of the Rising depicted the Sinn Féin stamps above the caption 'Stamps of the Irish Republic'.

With the outbreak of war in 1914 and the rise of more militant political movements, at first in Ulster and then throughout the country, official scrutiny passed from the stamps and addresses on letters to their content. Writing, by way of confidential circular in November 1915, to particular postmasters, Norway referred to 'seditious documents, books, pamphlets, leaflets, notices, etc. whether printed typed or written which it is desired to stop in the Post' and attached a long list of publications, many published in the United States, which must have been judged at least unpatriotic and potentially treasonable.[3] By warrant of the Lord Lieutenant, periodically renewed and amended in these years, the Secretary of the General Post Office, Dublin, was empowered 'to detain all copies of the said pamphlets, leaflets and notices which shall hereafter … be transmitted through the Post Office in Ireland, and to transmit the same to Our Under Secretary here for Our information.' Some were obvious anti-recruitment notices – *Irishmen don't enlist. Avoid the English Army, Navy and Police Forces* or the ballad 'It's a Wrong thing to fight for England'; others defiantly espouse the cause of Germany – *Germany's Just Cause* and *Germany's Hour of Destiny* – but a title like *Irish girls. Ireland has need of the loving service of all her children* defies immediate categorisation. For all such publications postmasters in the larger offices like Dublin, Cork, Belfast, Limerick and Queenstown – the last of crucial importance for the American mails – were enjoined to keep 'the most careful watch practicable, consistently [*sic*] with the due despatch of the Mails' and anything found 'in open packets or in the folds of newspapers' was to be sent up to the Secretary in Dublin 'under cover marked Confidential'.

---

3   An Post archives.

The Gaelic revival stimulated the use of Irish in correspondence giving rise to some operational and policy difficulties for the Post Office.
(Courtesy of the BPMA)

It comes as no surprise that, in the tumult of war abroad and political ferment at home, Norway should devote some consideration to the security of Post Office operations in Ireland and to the loyalty of his own staff. In the thoughtful and candid memoir which he wrote some ten years after the 1916 Rising, *Irish Experiences in War*, he is highly critical of what he saw as the government's failure to treat potential disloyalty in Ireland seriously and to avoid any action which might conceivably create friction. 'Everyone,' as he rather neatly puts it, 'believed that the point was off the Irish pikes, and the gunmen had forgotten how to shoot.'[4]

Faced with complacency, not only in London but also in the Irish Office in Dublin, Norway did his best to understand the nature of a burgeoning Irish renaissance that embraced the language and literature of the Gaelic League, the sport of the GAA as well as potentially serious political disaffection. In particular, he made discreet enquiries into an organisation about which he knew little,

4   'Irish Experiences in War', p. 4.

Cork GPO hurling team 1906. J. J. Walsh, a future Postmaster General (back row, 2nd left), and P. S. O'Hegarty, a future Secretary of the Department (middle row, 3rd left), are in the picture.

(An Post archives)

the Irish Republican Brotherhood, and which had been mentioned in the course of occasional police reports that reached his desk. Equally worrying to him was the increasing militancy in Ulster of Unionist opposition to Home Rule. It was the situation in Ulster, in fact, which first gave him cause to think about the relationship between Post Office servants and their political opinions. The only staff rule which seemed to touch on the matter was the injunction that 'Officers of the Post Office … should maintain a certain reserve in political matters, and not put themselves forward on one side or the other'. In considering whether signing the Ulster Covenant might have caused Post Office staff to breach this rule, Norway came to the conclusion that it did not and so advised the Postmaster General on the lines that:

> The Post Office does not proscribe political opinions of any type among its servants unless satisfied that such opinions are impairing the usefulness of the officer as a postal worker, or are prejudicial to the safety of the State.[5]

Having adopted this view in respect of the Ulster position, it made sense to apply it equally in the case of the formation of the Irish Volunteers.

It gradually became clear to Norway, however, that in the midst of increasing political tension throughout Ireland it might prove difficult to maintain in the minds of Post Office staff the necessary distinction between private political convictions and public duty. That the effects of such political tension might have ramifications beyond Ireland was impressed on him by the fact that the army confidentially briefed him over a year before the war broke out in 1914 on the line to be held if Ireland was invaded. In the circumstances, he drafted a short notice for staff, to be circulated to all post offices, making it clear that their political actions and opinions were in all cases to be subordinated to their duty to the Post Office. His attempt to clear the air on the matter, however, came to nothing for 'the Postmaster General thought the notice provocative, and others in London condemned it as unnecessary'.[6]

Neither the sound advice nor the confidential ear that he would have appreciated from his Post Office masters in London was forthcoming. They were simply not accustomed to having to think about such things, and his colleagues and acquaintances in Dublin tended to be firmly fixed in one camp or the other so

---

5   Given in evidence to the Royal Commission on the Rebellion in Ireland, see *Royal Commission on the Rebellion in Ireland: Minutes of Evidence*, p. 61.

6   'Irish Experiences in War', p. 7.

that, as he expressed it in one neatly turned phrase, 'consultation darkened counsel' and he was left to exercise his own judgement, doing his best to be fair to his staff and true to his duty to the Post Office.

The case of Patrick O'Keeffe, a Sorter Tracer in the Accounts Department, illustrates this. He was one of a few men who had been under police surveillance for some years, but Norway was not a man who automatically accepted all that was contained in the RIC files headed 'Dublin Extremists'. In response to information assembled by the special branch or G Division of the police, he wrote on 19 October 1914 that 'Mr O'Keeffe is an officer whose conduct is excitable and somewhat eccentric' – characteristics not unknown in the GPO over the years – but what caused Norway concern was the fact that he had 'broken the important rule which prohibits Post-Office servants taking a prominent part in politics' and O'Keeffe was duly reprimanded.[7]

Norway scrutinised the secret intelligence reports he received and separated suspect staff into three categories – 'Dangerous', 'Potentially dangerous' and 'Probably negligible'. By November 1914 he had compiled a record of slightly less than thirty names with only six people listed in the most serious class, placed there on police and army evidence that they were in regular communication with people known to be subversive. Anxious to receive some sort of guidance on the approach he was taking, he wrote twice to London enclosing his lists and explaining how they had been framed. No reply was sent to his first letter and the second memorandum, sent just three months before the Rising, elicited merely an acknowledgement that the matter was under consideration. London's reluctance, in the midst of war, to deal

---

7   United Kingdom National Archives, CO 904/196/62.

with delicate matters in Ireland is understandable, as indeed is
Norway's desire to seek instructions and to document the actions
he had taken. He must have been glad of the paper trail he created
at that time when he was later called to give evidence before the
Hardinge Commission.[8]

In that evidence, he points out that there was, in the case
of those known to be active members of the Irish Volunteers,
a change in the government's general policy of letting sleeping
dogs lie. In March 1915, at the instigation of the Irish Office, the
Postmaster General wrote a warning letter to eight Post Office
staff advising them that unless they ceased their connection with
the Volunteers, they would be liable to dismissal without further
notice.[9] The government at the time did not foresee insurrection,
but was focussed on the anti-recruitment activities of the people
concerned. In this context, the case of one postal sorter in
Waterford shows the difficulties Norway encountered in steering
the Irish Post Office through the growing political turbulence.
The man had been caught by soldiers in the act of tearing down
an army recruiting poster and his action was clearly incompatible
with his position as a civil servant. Norway fully expected his
dismissal but he found that charges were dropped by the army and
he was instructed that the man was to be reinstated with full pay
in his Post Office job. A local MP had let it be known that, should
any action be taken against the sorter, he would see to it that army

8   The Royal Commission on the Rebellion in Ireland was chaired by the
    diplomat and former Viceroy of India, Lord Hardinge of Penshurst.
9   This letter and the names of the Post Office staff are in Appendix 1.
    The initial draft refers in passing to the much larger group of National
    Volunteers from whom the Irish Volunteers had split over the issue
    of army recruitment. The Postmaster General deemed this reference
    'inexpedient' and it was removed. United Kingdom National Archives,
    CO 904/196/62.

recruitment in Waterford would be brought to an immediate stop. Norway's justifiable concern over the issue, which he took both to General Friend, commander-in-chief of the army in Ireland, and to Sir Mathew Nathan, was nothing compared with the government's insatiable demand for soldiers.

Another affair, the Swan Bar incident, took place on 24 May 1915, when Thomas Dolan, an engineering clerk in Aldborough House, and another couple of Post Office men expressed pro-German opinions while drinking porter in the Swan Bar. Their views gave offence to another customer and the barman and led to an altercation which continued on Aungier Street and down to Dame Street. A crowd gathered and arrests were made. This was a minor matter and there were doubtless similar incidents elsewhere, but one man whom Norway definitely regarded as dangerous was Cornelius Collins.

Another Sorter Tracer in the Accounts Department, Collins had been under police observation from at least 1911 and, since he was in regular contact with men who were at the heart of the nationalist movement, his activities were closely watched. Based in Dublin but with family connections in Limerick and a brother in the GPO in London, he was a man well placed to initiate contacts and convey news. Telegrams from the detectives assigned to watch him show how his departures and arrivals were monitored, but he was a man both shrewd and cool in his transactions. However, following one particular meeting the government felt that a case might be made against him and Sir Mathew Nathan wrote to Norway on 29 May 1915 pointing out that:

> Collins association with Lawlor ... believed to be still engaged in smuggling arms ... with T. J. Clarke and John McDermott ex convicts and with J. J. Walsh a Postal Official dismissed for disloyalty ... raise

the question whether action should not now be taken on the warning already given to him.[10]

Replying a few days later Norway is cautious and notes that:

> if the charge should prove to be inaccurate, the case against Mr. Collins is materially weakened, some of the incidents recorded being susceptible of natural explanations.

He goes on to refer to an interview he had had with Collins in which the man professed not to understand 'my references to association with persons engaged in movements hostile to the Government'. With a civil servant's reluctance to speak too plainly on such a matter, Norway records that he 'put the charge to him in general terms in the first instance, so as to see if he made any candid statement, such as an honest though indiscreet officer might wish to make.'[11] Collins was not to be caught out by such subtlety, however, and he managed to survive, despite Norway asking for his transfer to England right up to the evening of Good Friday 1916 when he was arrested (with thirty-five sovereigns and a revolver in his pocket) with Austin Stack in Tralee on a charge of conspiracy to land arms.

Norway's job in the year or so leading up to 1916 cannot have been easy. His immediate Post Office superiors lacked experience and understanding of the Irish question and readily sought the comfort of government assurances, suavely delivered by Chief Secretary Augustine Birrell, 'a shrewd literary critic, but a negligent and undiscerning politician', that all was well in Ireland. Sir Mathew Nathan who, given Birrell's reluctance to spend much time in Dublin,

10   United Kingdom National Archives, CO 904/196/62. J. J. Walsh returned to the Post Office as Postmaster General after independence.

11   *Ibid.*

was effectively in charge of matters at the Irish Office in Dublin Castle, wasn't much help either. While they knew each other well from the Post Office, they were temperamentally at odds, Norway being particularly critical of what he saw as Nathan's tendency to adopt, without qualification, the opinions and policies of his boss:

> His conception of loyalty was not to tell his political chief when he thought him wrong, but to help him in his policy without remonstrance – wherein, I think, he acted rather as becomes a soldier than a Civil Servant occupying an important post.[12]

For his part, Norway was undoubtedly a typical senior civil servant – efficient, traditional in outlook and rigidly apolitical. The business of his officials was the business of the postal service, and politics, in his view, had no place in the Sorting Office or telegraph room. That said, however, he strove to be scrupulously fair and saw no reason to believe that membership of Sinn Féin alone, for instance, 'rendered an officer less competent to serve the Postmaster General efficiently'.[13] Where, however, there was clear evidence of disloyalty he acted quickly. When suspicion fell, for instance, on a future Secretary of the Department of Posts and Telegraphs, P. S. O'Hegarty, who occupied the militarily sensitive postmastership of Queenstown (Cobh), Norway had him transferred. Since he was highly regarded in London and the evidence against him was insufficient,[14] O'Hegarty avoided dismissal. He, of course, turned out to have been an IRB man at the heart of the nationalist movement, and a wry smile must have crossed Norway's lips when

---

12 'Irish Experiences in War', p. 9.

13 *Ibid.*

14 P. S. O'Hegarty was transferred to Welshpool in north Wales in January 1915. His brother, Seán, also came under suspicion but he refused to be transferred and was consequently dismissed.

he saw him take over as first Secretary of the newly independent Irish Post Office in 1922.

It was not an easy time for staff who were drawn to politics, and one deputation from Cork sought a meeting with Norway to discuss the matter. It left with his assurance that, provided they were loyal to their duty, his staff would have his utmost support and that of the Post Office. Norway was respected for his plain dealing and it is much to his credit that in the months preceding the rebellion and during the soul searching which followed it, he did not waver in his commitment to protecting the interests of the Irish Post Office and its staff against unfair criticism and unjustified attack.

THE ATTACK ON THE GPO –
EASTER MONDAY, 24 APRIL 1916

The pleasant spring weather was a blessing for those free to enjoy the relaxed bank holiday atmosphere outside the GPO on Sackville Street on Easter Monday morning, but for those staff on duty inside it was a normal working day. Norway, who had left his wife and son Nevil in their temporary residence in the Royal Hibernian Hotel in Dawson Street,[1] had read the papers in his club and then gone in to his office to do some work in the relative calm of the bank holiday.[2] Not officially on duty, he was a diligent civil servant, keenly aware of his responsibility for the smooth running of the postal service in Ireland and his staff of just over 17,000 people. In comparison to his colleagues in London, his position called not merely for a firm grasp of postal operations but also for an ever-present and diplomatic sensitivity to the volatile political climate that obtained in Ireland.

It would have come as no surprise to Norway then to get a telephone call from Sir Matthew Nathan, soon after 11 a.m. that morning, asking him to drop up to the Castle. Dublin, he recalled a few days later in his first report to Sir Evelyn Murray, Post Office Secretary in London, appeared much as usual and, while the increasing armed strength of the Irish Volunteers had seemed to him to represent a 'serious danger', he had seen 'no reason to

---

1 Nevil Shute Norway was seventeen at the time and volunteered to serve as a Red Cross ambulance orderly during the Rising. He was awarded a certificate of honour by the St John's Ambulance brigade.
2 The Sackville Street Club was at 59 Upper Sackville Street, next door to the GPO Solicitor's Department.

The GPO and Nelson's Pillar before the Rising – an imposing prospect.

(An Post archives)

anticipate an outbreak' just then.[3] Leaving the GPO a mere quarter of an hour or so before its occupation by the Volunteer and Citizen Army contingent, he must often have wondered what would have happened if he had still been there in his office on the first floor of the GPO. He had in his drawer a loaded revolver that had belonged to his son Fred and which his younger son Nevil, well attuned perhaps to the increasing tension in the city, had persuaded him to keep handy. Writing in his private memoir, *Irish Experiences in War*, he wondered:

3   BPMA Post 56/177.

If I … had attempted, as I hope I should, to hold the staircase, I should
have been shot at once, and what is worse, I should have been blamed
by a frightened government seeking for a scapegoat.

Clearly, his experience of dealing with the British and Irish ad-
ministrations since his appointment to Dublin in 1912 must have
undermined somewhat the civil servant's customary reluctance to
criticise his political masters. 'Politicians in a difficulty,' he added,
'are never fair, and still less generous.'

At the outbreak of the First World War, Norway had seen the
vulnerability of the GPO telegraph network to destruction or
sabotage by a German agent or sympathiser. He had consequently
applied for and been given an armed guard for the telegraph room,
the sentries, he recalls, being under orders 'to keep their magazines
full … and … to shoot to stop any unidentified person who
approached the Instrument Room.'[4] Unfortunately, for reasons
and in circumstances unknown to him, the Instrument Room
guard was subsequently deprived of ammunition and left to stand
guard with empty rifles. 'The soldiers,' he writes, 'were helpless,
and the blame lies with those, probably civilians, who disarmed
them.'[5] Once again, there is a sense of deep frustration at what he
sees as government mismanagement of the Irish situation.

As Norway was making his way up to the Castle, a combined
Volunteer and Citizen Army force under Patrick Pearse and James
Connolly was preparing to march on the GPO. There are a number
of accounts of the occupation of the public office given by people
who took part in the event and they generally emphasise the
speed and efficiency with which the building was emptied, but the

4   'Irish Experiences in War', p. 25.
5   *Ibid.*

The new GPO Public Office opened shortly before the Rising.
(Courtesy of the National Library of Ireland)

The GPO Public Office after the Rising.
(Courtesy of the National Library of Ireland, Alb. 107)

GPO accounts do not confirm this. The public office was quickly cleared but the insurgents, perhaps preoccupied with fortifying the ground floor and reading the Proclamation, seem to have been rather lax in clearing the upper floors. The official reports made by the telegraph staff show that they did not leave the GPO until an hour after the Volunteers entered it.[6]

There must have been an initial feeling of incredulity, perhaps even amusement, which turned quickly to self-preservation as it became clear to staff and customers in the GPO that these armed men were in deadly earnest when they ordered the area to be cleared and took prisoner an off-duty soldier who was buying stamps.

Upstairs, in the telegraph office, Samuel Guthrie and his staff were not immediately aware of what was happening in the public office and the first indication that something was amiss probably came from telegraphists noticing that some line connections had inexplicably broken. There are a few different accounts covering this and it is worth turning to a couple to demonstrate how events unfolded from the perspective of those in the Telegraph Instrument Room.

William Pemberton, assistant superintendent, in his report to the Controller of Telegraphs, J. J. Kenny, wrote that at 12.23 p.m. (G) on Easter Monday:

Miss Brennan reported that all the stations on Switch 1 were

---

6   At first sight it seems that there is a serious and puzzling discrepancy between the timings given in the two accounts of the Telegraph Room's occupation, but this is explained when it is realised that one account is based on Greenwich (G) time and the other on Irish (I) or Dublin time. Dublin time, established under the Definition of Time Act in 1880, was abolished in October 1916 when wartime daylight-saving measures were introduced across the United Kingdom.

J. J. Kenny – Controller of the Telegraph Office in 1916.

(An Post archives)

disconnected. Mr Doak was speaking to me with ref to the Showyard Special wire which was also disconnected. On hearing Miss Brennan's report we thought the main batteries might be gone but having proved these right several of the lines were found to be disconnected including the Cross-channel circuits. I got the key of the Secondary Cell Room and with Mr Doak proceeded to the basement and examined the heat coil pane which appeared to be all right. I returned to the Instrument Room and … suggested that ex Sergeant Connell should accompany Mr Doak to the basement to make further examination of the Heat Coil Frame.[7]

7   BPMA Post 31/80B, Pemberton to Kenny in his report of 6 May 1916.

Kenny, the Controller, was at home that day but he got a call shortly before 12.30 to inform him that 'all the wires had gone "dis" (telegraph and telephone) except the Southern lines'.[8] A few minutes later, he got a further message with the news that 'the Volunteers had entered the Post Office and had taken over the Public Counter'. A little later again came the information, relayed by Mr P. I. Kelly, sorting clerk and telegraphist, that 'the Sinn Feiners were in the Instrument Room, that all the staff had been ordered out, and that he would have to leave the building immediately.'[9] The internet, live relays and 'breaking news' commentaries of our own day have rather dulled our senses to the excitement of receiving news as it happens and we need to remember that it must have been a quite extraordinary situation for Kenny to have details of the attack relayed to him on the phone from the GPO.

In his absence, Samuel Guthrie, the superintendent, was in charge. Guthrie, who had been Kenny's boss at one stage, was a very experienced officer whose career in the Post Office had begun in Ballybrophy over forty-five years before. His account of the attack on the Instrument Room on the second floor of the GPO is of great interest and reveals that the occupation of the GPO was not achieved quite as easily or as quickly as has been generally thought. It is worth turning to his account for a description of events:

At 12 noon (I) a great many of the wires – including all the cross channel wires – became disconnected, apparently close up. At 12.10 p.m. I was informed that the Sinn Fein Volunteers were taking possession of the Public Counter and after a short time I heard the breaking of glass

8   In standard telegraph usage 'dis' means disconnected.
9   BPMA Post 31/80B, Kenny to Norway in his report of 12 May 1916.

in the lower storey. On looking out of a window in the Telephone Room I saw that the windows of the Public Office and other windows looking into Sackville Street were being smashed, the fragments of glass falling on to and covering the pavement, and several members of the Sinn Fein party stood round the public entrance with rifles and revolvers. I at once got Mr P. I. Kelly to 'phone to Headquarters of the Army Command, the Police Office in the Castle, and also to Marlboro' Barracks asking for assistance.[10]

Figure 1 (overleaf) should help to clarify the location of the Instrument Room and the position of the Telephone Room from which Guthrie was able to look out and see the glass falling from the smashed windows. One of the women looking on from Sackville Street is quoted as saying, 'Glory be to God. The divils are smashing all the lovely windows' and her indignation would have touched a chord with those looking down from Guthrie's window.[11]

Once the Public Office had been cleared, a Volunteer party headed upstairs to continue the task of emptying the building and we can turn again to Guthrie for help in picturing the scene:

At 12.30 p.m. I was informed by the Sergt. of the Guard that the Rebels were forcing the stairs leading from Henry Street to the Instrument Room and he asked me to obtain assistance for him. I explained to him what we had already done to obtain assistance. The guard consisted of a Sergeant and 4 men. The passage leading from the head of the stairs to the Instrument Room was then barricaded from the inside by filling it with chairs, wastepaper boxes etc. in order to delay the entry of the attackers as much as possible, the guard of 1

10 BPMA Post 31/80B, Guthrie to Kenny in his report of 6 May 1916.
11 W. J. Brennan-Whitmore, *Dublin Burning*, p. 39.

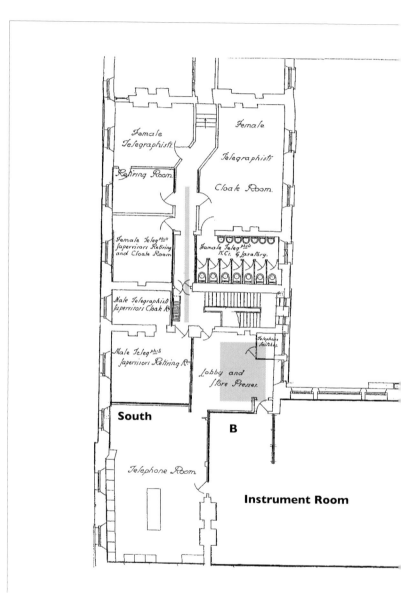

Figure 1. Floor-plan of the second storey of the GPO.

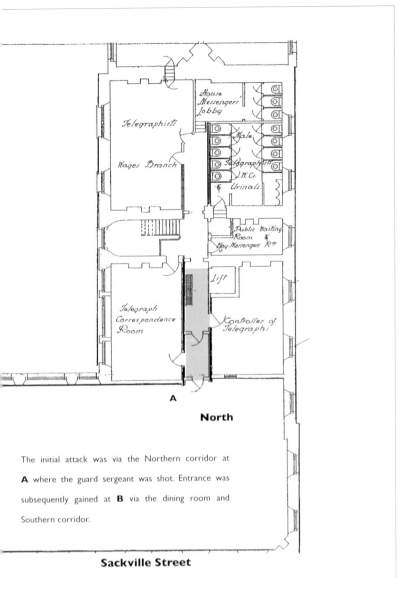

North

The initial attack was via the Northern corridor at **A** where the guard sergeant was shot. Entrance was subsequently gained at **B** via the dining room and Southern corridor.

Sackville Street

(An Post archives)

Sergeant and 4 men standing inside the Instrument Room prepared to
receive the rebels if they broke through the obstructions.[12]

The military guard on the telegraph room seems to have done
all that it could to prevent the entry of the attacking Volunteers.
Pemberton's account of the situation adds the detail that the guard,
though lacking ammunition for their guns, fixed bayonets and
stood on either side of the northern entrance door to withstand
the attack. The attacking party did not, it would seem, enter into
any discussion at this stage but attempted instead to force an
entrance through the corridor leading to the Instrument Room.
'Several volleys,' records Guthrie, 'were fired by the Rebels through
the passage into the Instrument Room' and Pemberton is able to
add that he 'saw the Sergt. stagger as if wounded'. The resistance
offered at this end of the Instrument Room may have prompted
the Volunteers to send another group to attack by the southern
door. This strategy proved more successful and, writes Guthrie:

A short time before 1 p.m. a party of the Rebels gained an entrance to
the Instrument Room by the Southern Corridor after having passed
through the Dining Room. As there was only one sentry on that
corridor he was easily overpowered.[13]

Guthrie must have been a worried man, but as the attack began on
the northern corridor, he did his best to shield the female staff there
from the shooting, instructing them to 'go into their Retiring Room'
and, with rather touching avuncular concern in the circumstances,
to 'put on their outdoor apparel in case they would have to leave
the building'. The female staff, however, were not without their own

---

12 BPMA Post 31/80B, Guthrie to Kenny in his report of 6 May 1916.
13 *Ibid.*

local heroine in the form of Miss Gordon, Assistant Supervisor Telegraphs, whom Pemberton notes:

> declined to leave the Instrument Room when the rebels occupied it until she had attended to the wounds of the Sergeant of the Military Guard, who had been injured in his plucky effort to defend the Southern entrance to the room.[14]

The sergeant's wounds were more than superficial and the two, having given their word to return to the GPO, were permitted to go down to Jervis Street hospital to receive professional attention. True to their promise, they did return and, while the sergeant was kept a prisoner, Miss Gordon, having shown both bravery and compassion for a fellow Scot, was allowed to leave the building at about 5 o'clock.

Guthrie's old-fashioned gallantry in relation to his female staff is in keeping with his attitude to those who had attacked the Post Office. Informed that an officer of the besieging force wanted to see him about the withdrawal of his staff, he 'sent word to him that I would not hold any parley with him as I did not recognise he had any right to be where he was'. The officer, subsequently identified as The O'Rahilly, and accompanied by a few supporters, entered the Instrument Room a few minutes later 'each carrying a revolver and told all the officials in the Room to clear out at once at the same time questioning each one as to whether he carried arms'.[15] Pemberton's account once again adds a touch of colour to the older man's more formal narrative:

---

14 BPMA Post 31/80B, Pemberton to Kenny in his report of 6 May 1916.
15 BPMA Post 31/80B, Guthrie to Kenny in his report of 6 May 1916. Guthrie's typescript identifies the officer as 'a Mr Connolly' but this has been crossed out and replaced with 'The O'Rahilly'.

A rebel ordered us out of the building with the remark 'sorry to disturb you gentlemen' and made some additional remark like 'this is the first and last act'.[16]

The female staff had already left the room and by 1.31 p.m. (G) the men were on their way down stairs to be 'let out of the main gate at Prince's Street by the rebel guard'. Pemberton immediately made his way to Brunswick Street[17] police station to report the matter, but the police there, displaying a rather remarkable lack of interest, redirected him to Store Street, telling him to make his report there.

A fire-proof cable chamber which remarkably survived the intense heat of the GPO fires.

(Courtesy of the National Library of Ireland, Alb. 107)

16 BPMA Post 31/80B, Pemberton to Kenny in his report of 6 May 1916.
17 Now Pearse Street.

The Proclamation – Justifying the Rising

The Post Office staff magazine, *St Martin's-Le-Grand*, a well-written compilation of staff news, items of Post Office significance and articles of general interest, contains a couple of accounts of the occupation of the GPO. One of these, unsigned but composed by one of the staff in the Telegraph Instrument Room upstairs, records that from the windows some rebels could be seen guarding the entrance to the public counter 'whilst others were distributing to a crowd large poster sheets which proved to be copies of the Proclamation of the Irish Republic'.[1] The 1916 leaders were conscious that they needed to have some sort of statement prepared which might justify the militant, undemocratic step they were taking and one of Patrick Pearse's first actions was to come to the front of the building and proclaim the Irish Republic a sovereign, independent state. His few listeners, attracted by the activity on a quiet bank holiday, heard him with a somewhat bemused indifference, unaware that they were witnessing the beginning of events that would profoundly influence Irish history. Today, nearly a century later, a copy of that Proclamation is on display in the An Post Museum just a few yards from the spot where Pearse first read out the famous opening words 'Irishmen and Irishwomen'.

Solemn and high-minded in tone, the Proclamation is thought to be largely the work of Pearse, but there is a radical edge to the content – guarantees of religious and civil liberty, equal rights and opportunities for all citizens and votes for women as well as men – which points to the influence of James Connolly, the labour leader

---

1 *St Martin's-Le-Grand*, 1916.

POBLACHT NA H EIREANN.

THE PROVISIONAL GOVERNMENT
OF THE
IRISH REPUBLIC
TO THE PEOPLE OF IRELAND.

IRISHMEN AND IRISHWOMEN : In the name of God and of the dead generations from which she receives her old tradition of nationhood, Ireland, through us, summons her children to her flag and strikes for her freedom.

Having organised and trained her manhood through her secret revolutionary organisation, the Irish Republican Brotherhood, and through her open military organisations, the Irish Volunteers and the Irish Citizen Army, having patiently perfected her discipline, having resolutely waited for the right moment to reveal itself, she now seizes that moment, and, supported by her exiled children in America and by gallant allies in Europe, but relying in the first on her own strength, she strikes in full confidence of victory.

We declare the right of the people of Ireland to the ownership of Ireland, and to the unfettered control of Irish destinies, to be sovereign and indefeasible.   The long usurpation of that right by a foreign people and government has not extinguished the right, nor can it ever be extinguished except by the destruction of the Irish people.   In every generation the Irish people have asserted their right to national freedom and sovereignty : six times during the past three hundred years they have asserted it in arms.   Standing on that fundamental right and again asserting it in arms in the face of the world, we hereby proclaim the Irish Republic as a Sovereign Independent State, and we pledge our lives and the lives of our comrades-in-arms to the cause of its freedom, of its welfare, and of its exaltation among the nations.

The Irish Republic is entitled to, and hereby claims, the allegiance of every Irishman and Irishwoman.   The Republic guarantees religious and civil liberty, equal rights and equal opportunities to all its citizens, and declares its resolve to pursue the happiness and prosperity of the whole nation and of all its parts, cherishing all the children of the nation equally, and oblivious of the differences carefully fostered by an alien government, which have divided a minority from the majority in the past.

Until our arms have brought the opportune moment for the establishment of a permanent National Government, representative of the whole people of Ireland and elected by the suffrages of all her men and women, the Provisional Government, hereby constituted, will administer the civil and military affairs of the Republic in trust for the people.

We place the cause of the Irish Republic under the protection of the Most High God, Whose blessing we invoke upon our arms, and we pray that no one who serves that cause will dishonour it by cowardice, inhumanity, or rapine.   In this supreme hour the Irish nation must, by its valour and discipline and by the readiness of its children to sacrifice themselves for the common good, prove itself worthy of the august destiny to which it is called.

Signed on Behalf of the Provisional Government,

THOMAS J. CLARKE,
SEAN Mac DIARMADA,   THOMAS MacDONAGH,
P. H. PEARSE,   EAMONN CEANNT,
JAMES CONNOLLY.   JOSEPH PLUNKETT.

The 1916 Proclamation – justification, exhortation and declaration in equal measure.

(An Post archives)

and founder of the Irish Citizen Army. The document, therefore, is more than a justification and a call to arms: it is a statement of belief and a vision of a better future for all Irish men and women.

The final wording of the Proclamation was agreed at a meeting in the old Liberty Hall in Abbey Street on Easter Sunday morning and later that day two compositors and a printer began work there on the 2,500 print run. Theirs was a dangerous task and their conditions were difficult: they had to struggle with an old and dilapidated printing press, inferior paper and insufficient type. Shortage of type meant that the Proclamation had to be printed in two halves. This is immediately apparent from the marked contrast between the lightly inked top half of the document and the more heavily inked bottom half. The men printed the top half, redistributed their type and set it again for the bottom half. The half-printed sheets were reinserted into the press and the lower portion added to that already printed.

Certain letters, notably 'e', were in short supply and different fonts had to be used. What looks like a capital E in the fifth line, TO THE, is actually an F with an additional leg, made from sealing wax, joined on to it! As a sample of their art, the printers might have been less than happy with the Proclamation but, in terms of patience and ingenuity under difficult and dangerous conditions, it must rank as a very accomplished piece of work. It was the early hours of Easter Monday morning before they had their work done and copies ready for distribution around the city later in the day.[2]

The Proclamation is a rare document with very few copies known to have survived. Each has individual associations, with An Post's copy, for instance, bearing in the top left-hand corner the

2   On the printing of the Proclamation, see J. J. Bouch's article in *Publications of the Bibliographical Society of Ireland*, Vol. 5, No. 3.

inscription 'Found in Dublin Easter 1916 by John Phillips'. Min Ryan, later to marry Richard Mulcahy, was in and out of the GPO a few times during the week and on Thursday took with her three copies which she gave to the wives of the leaders. One participant in the Rising, later destined to become President of Ireland, was Seán T. O'Kelly. He was given the dangerous and responsible job of pasting up the Proclamations around the city centre. Realising, perhaps, that not many of them might survive the turmoil, he put his trust in the Post Office and posted one to his aunt, in the pillar-box a few yards from the GPO itself. With a little understandable delay, it was duly delivered and survives to this day.

In 1916 this large lower window was the main GPO doorway from which Pearse emerged to read the Proclamation.

(Stephen Ferguson)

Breaking the News –
Amiens Street station

While Pearse, Connolly and Tom Clarke were busy fortifying the GPO, Sam Guthrie and the other displaced telegraph staff were making it known that something very odd was happening in Dublin. During the few minutes he had before the Instrument Room was taken over by the occupying contingent, Guthrie had done his best to summon help and inform the government of what was happening. The senior officers at Army Headquarters in Parkgate were absent, but the acting officer, Colonel Cowan, reacted promptly by despatching troops to reinforce Dublin Castle and secure the Viceregal Lodge. It is also clear that Guthrie's staff got through to Richmond Barracks and that troops were sent to the aid of staff in the GPO.[1] The well-known deployment of the Lancers, though in keeping with standard military strategy of the time, was in retrospect a mistake and led to the first exchange of fire in the Rising when the Volunteers opened fire on them from the GPO.

Aware at this stage that the wires to England must have been deliberately cut, Guthrie, once evicted from the GPO, met up with Mr H. Doak, Assistant Engineer, and together they made their way down to Amiens Street (Connolly) railway station to see if they could get through to London from the post office telegraph office there. Pemberton, the Assistant Superintendent who had been told by the police in Brunswick Street to make his report in Store Street, was already there with a few of the displaced telegraph operators from the GPO. Since one of the cross-channel cables from the GPO

1   See G. A. Hayes-McCoy's essay on the military aspects of the Rising in *The Making of 1916*, edited by Kevin B. Nowlan.

The message sent by Doak and Guthrie from Amiens Street, via Wales, on Easter Monday.

(Courtesy of the BPMA)

ran through the Amiens Street station telegraph office, Guthrie and the engineers were able to pass on the news of the attack to London. A service message routed from Dublin (DN) to London, via the telegraph relay station at Nevin (NV) in Wales, conveys the first news of the Rising in telegraphically laconic style:

> DN informs NV that Volunteers have taken possession of Telegraph Office at DN. And all lines stopped in consequence.[2]

A little later came another message sent by Edward Gomersall, the Superintending Engineer, to the Secretary, Sir Evelyn Murray, in London:

> GPO Dublin taken possession of today at noon by Sinn Feiners – Sorting Office and Instrument Room wrecked. Some railway stations also held.[3]

---

2   BPMA Post 14/336.
3   *Ibid.*

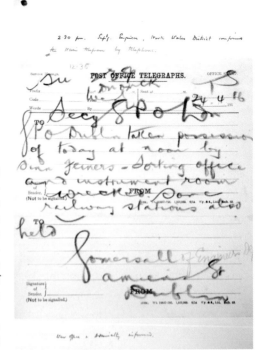

Sent by Edward Gomersall, Superintending Engineer in Dublin, to the GPO Secretary in London, this telegram relays the startling news of Sinn Féin rebellion in Dublin.

(Courtesy of the BPMA)

Guthrie called the Central Telegraph Office in London:

I am speaking from Amiens St Rl. The GPO has been taken possession of by the Volunteers … and I am afraid they are bent on demolishing the inst. room. I tell you in case you may have wondered why you could not get DN. Will you please advise Secretary and anyone else that it may concern and also advise any Irish Stns. it may be right to … I will take Govt. work and will do best to deliver it. The streets are not safe.[4]

Even though the streets were not safe, Guthrie tried to contact Norway at his residence in the Royal Hibernian Hotel, but when

4   *Ibid.*

he arrived there he was told that Norway was probably stuck at Dublin Castle. He headed back down to Amiens Street and, on the suggestion of the London Telegraph Superintendent, despatched Pemberton and a telegraphist, Mr Boyle, to make some necessary adjustments to the Nevin connection telegraph wires at Newcastle Hut, an unmanned telegraph cable building in County Wicklow. Since Westland Row and Harcourt Street stations were both 'in the hands of the Rebels', he empowered Pemberton to secure a 'motor car at Thompsons or some other garage'.[5] With races on at Fairyhouse and all the cars already engaged, Pemberton, who couldn't himself drive, had great difficulty in finding transport. His narrative, which includes dealing with people who found his story hard to believe, satisfactorily establishing his own identity and politely declining the assistance of a lady driver in case he brought her into danger, begins to read like the script of an early Charlie Chaplin comedy but, in the end, they got to Bray where they found thirty-six lines cut between Bray and Bray Head.

The quick establishment of the communications link through Amiens Street railway telegraph office by the Post Office engineering and telegraph staff was vital to the government. By Monday night the available engineering and telegraphy staff had managed to rig up a military telegraph line between Dublin and London and another between the government's Irish Office in Dublin Castle and its counterpart in London. As there was no existing connection between the Castle and Amiens Street, the connection was made by means of a telephone line through the Crown Alley Telephone Exchange, which had been left undisturbed by the Dublin insurgents. Superintending Engineer

---

5   BPMA Post 31/80B, Guthrie to Kenny in his report of 6 May 1916. The Thomson Motor Car Co., motor engineers and hirers, had premises at 19 and 20 Great Brunswick Street.

The temporary Telegraph Instrument Room installed in the Drawing
Room of the GNR's premises at Amiens Street station during the Rising.
(Courtesy of the National Library of Ireland. Alb. 107.)

Gomersall himself drove around the city outskirts and restored
communications by picking up and rerouting damaged cables via
private circuits. By late afternoon GPO staff were relaying civil
and military telegrams, giving news of the rebellion.

Shortly after 6 p.m. on Easter Monday, Nathan, the Under
Secretary, had been able to inform his boss, Augustine Birrell, of
events in Dublin: 'Insurrection broke out noon today in Dublin'
he begins and after giving some details of casualties and positions
occupied, concludes with a nice touch of understatement: 'Situation
at present not satisfactory'.[6] Army command (Commandeth
Dublin in telegraphic language) sent an update on the situation
to General Headquarters, Home Forces, Horse Guards, London,

6   BPMA Post 14/336.

just before 9 p.m., reporting on the positions held by insurgent and government forces and giving the news that 1,600 troops had arrived from the Curragh and that 'four eighteen-pounder guns were on their way from Athlone'. 'There has been some looting' the message concludes and 'casualties up to present under fifty'.

Heavy firing around Amiens Street, which had been going on for some time, continued into the early hours of Tuesday morning with Commandeth Dublin reporting at 8.25 a.m. that 'Insurgents are strengthening Sackville Street on both sides to command Post Office' and noting that 'Insurgents scattered in houses will not come out in open'. Towards noon Commandeth sent another telegram to army headquarters in London (Cinchomfor Ldn.) informing them that they would not be 'attacking their main strength in Sackville Street about GPO till reinforcements arrive'. The telegraph office at Amiens Street station was dangerously exposed, so Doak obtained agreement from the engineer of the Great Northern Railway to use the GNR's premises where a large Drawing Room, containing broad benches suitable for telegraph apparatus, was turned into a temporary telegraph office.[7] By the morning of Wednesday 26 April then, just two days after the start of the Rising, a replacement telegraph office had been established in the Drawing Room of the GNR's Amiens Street headquarters with four lines to London, one to Liverpool and one to Belfast. Following an instruction received the day before from the Secretary Telegraphs London ordering all private and press telegrams to be held, the available lines were wholly at the disposal of the civil and military authorities.

As the fighting and fires intensified during the week, the Post

---

7   F. A. Campion, Engineer-in-Chief of the Great Northern Railway Company.

Office staff in Amiens Street showed remarkable composure, continuing to work steadily in dangerous circumstances. Guthrie had been able to get home on the Monday and Tuesday nights, but he had to circumvent street fighting on his way in on Wednesday morning and by that evening the relief staff, Messrs Sweeney and Doyle, Assistant Superintendents, were unable to get through at all. 'As the whole city became involved in the disturbances,' he reported, 'all travelling through the street was practically suspended and remained so up to Sunday the 30th.'[8] Virtually isolated from Wednesday morning until the following Sunday, Guthrie and his colleagues concentrated on maintaining and protecting the essential communications links with London, Liverpool and Belfast. He remained on duty until noon on 1 May.

Gomersall, the engineering chief, and his staff had been concentrating on maintaining communication lines throughout the country as well as the cross-channel connections. He scribbled a quick note to Norway on Wednesday 26 April summarising his work in repairing the disruption caused by the attacks carried out on the telegraph lines on Monday morning. He had put in trunk telephone circuits to the Curragh and to Maryborough (Portlaoise), where he was 'endeavouring to get more circuits'. He had repaired links with Waterford and the south-eastern counties where 'a little damage was done: but it has been remedied'. He hoped to restore telegram links for the south-west by opening an office at Kingsbridge (Heuston) while 'in the meantime any urgent official messages may be handed to the Railway Telegraph office' there.[9] Arrangements were also strengthened by the establishment of a telegraph office at Broadstone railway station.

8   BPMA Post 31/80B, Guthrie to Kenny in his report of 6 May 1916.
9   BPMA Post 56/177.

CROWN ALLEY
TELEPHONE EXCHANGE

A decisive blow to the operations of the Volunteers was their failure to capture the Central Telephone Exchange in Crown Alley. The planning which had led to the successful severing of telegraph lines in the city and on several railway lines indicates their clear appreciation of the strategic importance of disrupting government communication channels and the Telephone Exchange was on the list of targets for Easter Monday. On the day, however, there were insufficient men to carry out the planned destruction of the cabling manhole in Crown Alley. Martin King, a Post Office cable joiner was ready to do so, but in a statement to the Bureau of Military History he stated that 'the Volunteers detailed for the Telephone Exchange did not turn up for the job on Easter Monday so I reported to the Citizen Army Garrison at the College of Surgeons.'[1] A detachment subsequently sent to occupy the Exchange was put off by a report that it was heavily protected by soldiers.[2] This was not, in fact, the case and Norway, once the Rising had begun, applied early on to Nathan for an increased guard on the Exchange. With the Exchange under government control, Post Office engineering staff were able to circumvent the wires that had been cut and, by means of the Amiens Street and Kingsbridge telegraph offices, maintain the lines that would ensure a strong and co-ordinated response to the insurrection.

---

1   BMH WS 0543.
2   Max Caulfield in *The Easter Rebellion* (revised edition 1995) p. 69 suggests that it was an old woman shouting, 'Go back, boys, go back, the place is crammed with military!' that prevented the capture of the Exchange.

Crown Alley Telephone Exchange – the 'plucky' conduct, under sustained rebel fire, of the telephonists here drew particular praise from Post Office management.

(Stephen Ferguson)

The work involved in this was not only highly dangerous for the engineering staff, but also technically challenging, and Norway's chief engineer, Edward Gomersall, recorded something of the difficulties faced by his staff in a short piece he wrote for *The Post Office Electrical Engineers' Journal* in July 1916.[3] He knew of at least sixty places, excluding damage to equipment inside Dublin city and suburbs, where telephone and telegraph lines had been

3   I am grateful to Mr Tom Wall, formerly Museum Keeper and Archivist at Eircom, for kindly drawing my attention to this article.

cut. Nearly all the main lines close to Dublin had been severed, generally in more than one place, the method adopted being:

> … to cut down two or three, sometimes more poles, and to cut the wires. At many places telegraph and telephone instruments were removed from the office and smashed to pieces in the road; block and electric train staff instruments and telephone and telegraph apparatus in signal boxes were battered and destroyed.[4]

When Gomersall's staff began to divert the telegraph wires to temporary offices, they found that most of the underground telegraph and telephone trunk cables had been cut, and Gomersall mentions that he himself had in his possession a 'cheap tenon saw' which had been found in one of the manholes where the lines had been cut and which, 'though not of Post Office pattern', had proved nonetheless quite adequate for the job that was done. The equipment necessary, including duplicate keys, had been collected by rebels before the Rising and stored in Liberty Hall.

The methodical nature in which a great many lines were cut by the rebels highlights not only their technical expertise, based on information and assistance from a few Post Office sympathisers, but also their clear understanding of the strategic significance of the Post Office's communications network. It emphasises, at the same time, just how serious a blow to their cause was the failure to capture the Crown Alley Telephone Exchange. The historian of the Post Office Engineering Union attributes that failure to the prompt action of two union members, J. McDonnell and S. A. Verschoyle, in notifying the military authorities of the need to protect the Exchange.[5] No conclusions must be drawn, however,

---

4   E. Gomersall, 'Irish Rebellion, 1916', in *The Post Office Electrical Engineers' Journal,* Vol. IX, July 1916.

5   Frank Bealey, *The Post Office Engineering Union,* p. 126.

on the general loyalty of union members, since two of their union colleagues, A. J. Fitzpatrick and James Byrne, both of whom were clerical assistants in the Engineering Department, were deported to Knutsford in Cheshire with other suspected Volunteers after the Rising.

While Gomersall and his assistants braved bullets – in one instance summoning doctor, priest and ambulance for a dying man – in their efforts to repair cables and restore telegraph circuits, the girls in the Telephone Exchange relayed telegraph messages over Crown Alley's intact telephone lines. The staff on duty when the Rising started were besieged in the building and had no opportunity to go home or be relieved by other staff. Sniper fire entered through the windows and bullets passed close to the girls who manned the telephones. The switch board casing was removed from the back of the telephones and used as a barricade to afford them some protection, and the few men in the building took over at night to let the women snatch a few hours' rest on mattresses in the basement. The hastily summoned military presence ensured that, while the rebels would be unlikely to capture the Exchange after they had lost their initial opportunity, the building continued to draw fire from rebel positions nearby. With food short, sleep difficult and danger ever-present, the Crown Alley staff must have felt themselves transported to some field communications position on the Western Front.

It is no surprise that Norway, writing on 30 April in his report to Murray, singles out for particular mention the bravery of the 'twenty girls who maintained the telephone service for six days amid sounds of fighting'.[6] Their 'wonderful pluck' in circumstances of 'indisputable personal danger' draws his admiration and he

6   BPMA Post 56/177.

suggests to Murray that he would find it hard, without coming over to Dublin himself, to appreciate just how much the Post Office owed to them. About forty staff, adding in the male employees, remained in the Exchange from Wednesday 26 April until the end of hostilities and stuck to their posts even when bullets entered the switchroom itself.

The press seized on the role of the telephone girls as an example of exceptional courage and devotion to duty, and the response of the Post Office to their actions was seen as both inadequate and dilatory. The *Irish Independent* carried a letter complaining that 'the greatest revenue-producing department of the State' had still not paid the overtime pay earned by the Exchange staff and reported a rumour that the overtime pay was itself to be reduced by an amount to cover the cost of hiring the mattresses! 'Could anything equal this as a sample of official cheeseparing at the expense of a poorly-paid class of Civil Servants?' the writer continued. He acknowledged that the Post Office Secretary had personally visited the Exchange and thanked the staff for their loyal and effective service, but 'soft words butter no parsnips' and it was time, he concluded, 'to see some practical value attached to official words of praise and thanks'. [7]

The 'cheeseparing' example of deducting a sum for mattress hire was doubtless just a rumour but a convincing enough one, nonetheless, for the Post Office, though fair, was not a generous employer. In due course, the Exchange staff duly received their overtime pay and an extra leave allowance in accordance with the general recommendation put forward by Norway for approval by London after the Rising.

---

7   *Irish Independent*, 5 July 1916.

Dublin Castle

In Dublin Castle on the morning of Easter Monday 1916, J. J. Fogarty and L. W. Galbally, postal telegraphists, were on duty working on government telegraph traffic. Shortly after the Rising, on 3 May 1916, Fogarty wrote up an official diary note of events at the Castle during the week. His record, once again, provides an invaluable first-hand account of what actually happened during the attack on the Castle and gives an answer as to why that attack was not pressed home at the time.

Fogarty arrived at the office at 9.35 a.m. where he was kept busy by a large number of police reports about railway lines cut by the Irish Volunteers and by a long message from the Under Secretary, Sir Mathew Nathan, to the Chief Secretary, Augustine Birrell, in London. Suddenly, at about 12.10 p.m. he heard several shots outside the office and looked out to see the unfortunate policeman who was on duty at the gate lying on the ground:

> Five or six Irish Volunteers in green uniform could be seen firing from Castle Street at the Guard who withdrew inside the Guard Room, one of the sentries half shutting the large gate.[1]

The Volunteers made their way through the gate and, while two or three tried to enter the Guard Room, the others came right into the middle of the Castle yard. Watching all this, Fogarty naturally felt it was high time to seek instructions from the Under Secretary and he recalls:

> as I crossed the hall the policeman on duty shut the door with a loud

---

1   BPMA Post 31/80B, *Diary Notes of work performed by Postal Telegraphists at Dublin Castle during the insurrection.*

bang the report of which startled the Volunteers (about 4 in number) who quickly withdrew from the Castle and joined by others entered the City Hall.

Was it the loud bang of a slammed door, mistaken for a shot, which prevented the occupation of the Castle and the likely capture of the Under Secretary?

Fogarty was unable to find Nathan so he rang Military Head-quarters at Parkgate and reported the attack on the Castle to Major Owen Lewis. He contacted Ship Street and Portobello Barracks and discovered they had also been attacked, but he was unable to get through to Marlborough, Beggars Bush or the Royal Barracks. At 12.30 p.m. he got a message from the GPO asking him to report the attack on the Post Office and over the next ten minutes calls came from 'various places (Four Courts, Jacobs, Distillery and Railway Stations) reporting attacks by Sinn Feiners'. About 12.50 the Castle telegraphists lost contact with the GPO.

Outside the Castle some Volunteers could be seen making their way across the roof of the City Hall while others were observed in the Municipal Buildings across the street 'exactly in front of our room'. Just after 1 p.m. Fogarty saw a car drive up to the side entrance of the City Hall:

> with 4 or 5 Volunteers and 1 woman dressed in green in it. They handed out many rifles and ammunition to those already in City Hall and were about to hand out more when Major Price came up from R.I.C. Office and fired a revolver at them. He appeared to hit one man who fell forward in car which was then rapidly driven away.[2]

---

2   Major Ivor Price was an RIC County Inspector who had been seconded as Intelligence Officer to the Irish Command at the start of the First World War.

With no defensive force in the Castle, the small band there 'breathed more freely' when at 2.30 some fifty or sixty soldiers from Portobello Barracks (RIR and Dublin Fusiliers) arrived and a further half company which 'had to fight all the way down' an hour later. From 3 p.m. there was a constant exchange of shots between the Volunteers and the army, but the military felt too weak to venture an attack as the surrounding buildings were 'in the hands of the rebels who had snipers on every roof'. At 7 p.m. large numbers of reinforcements from the Curragh and other places started to arrive and a machine gun was placed in the room above them. It opened fire on the City Hall at 9 p.m. 'demolishing most of the lower windows' and by 10 p.m. the building had been stormed and cleared.

Earlier in the afternoon Fogarty had managed to contact a chemist near his home in Donnybrook in order to tell his wife 'not to expect me for a long time'. He hadn't eaten since breakfast time, but 'managed to get Tea from resident Messenger who had barely enough to go round for us all including some officers'. Work for himself and his colleague was very difficult, with six of their nine Exchange lines having been cut earlier in the day. The remainder were subject to 'heavy overhearing' and 'it was only by getting the Operator to keep cutting in so as to see if lines clear that calls could be effected'. As evening fell, it became hard to see what they were doing since it was too dangerous to put on the light. 'On one occasion we flickered the light for a second and a shot entered the room next ours'. By removing all but the switch board bulb, which they obscured with the aid of brown paper and a heavy screen, they managed to get just enough light by which to work. Interrupted by military messages throughout the night, they gave up any attempt to settle to sleep on the floor.

Located at the historic heart of British government in Ireland

and exposed to hostile fire within a few yards of where they were working, the Castle telegraphists were in more immediate danger than most other Post Office staff in the opening days of the Rising and Fogarty's notes certainly bear this out. His diary entry for Tuesday conjures up a picture of peril at every corner:

> Earlier the troops had occupied the Municipal Buildings & were firing at the Volunteers on the Mail Offices and Parliament Street, but a machine gun on the roof of Henry & James gave them a lot of trouble. Round the Lower Yard bullets came from every direction, snipers being on the roof of Pims & the houses in Stephen Street & Ship Street. Some also came from further off, probably Jacobs, and others from Dame Lane and Dame St.[3]

In the midst of all this it must have taken quite some courage to cross the Castle yard to see the Under Secretary about his telegrams to London!

Galbally, in comparison, makes the whole experience sound rather dull:

> The work at this office varied very little from day to day and consisted in taking messages for Amiens Street T.O. for the Royal Irish Constabulary and work from the Irish Office (via Amiens Street) for the Chief Secretary's Office.[4]

Perhaps he lacked his colleague's awareness that history was being made, although it is only fair to say that Galbally was writing an official report and not a personal memoir.

---

3   BPMA Post 31/80B, *Diary Notes*. Henry & James, a clothing firm, occupied premises on the corner of Parliament Street and Dame Street. Pim Brothers, a large department store, was at the bottom of George's Street and survived to delight later generations of children with a memorable Santa ride at Christmas.

4   *Ibid.*

Fogarty and Galbally remained on duty until the following Monday. Constantly occupied with telegram and telephone messages, unable to sleep for more than a couple of hours at a time and short of food – 'we got some biscuits and two tins of beef from the military which we found very acceptable' – they certainly earned their overtime pay. Fogarty finally left the office at 4.10 p.m. on Monday 1 May, 'feeling almost too tired to walk', but boyishly satisfied that he had 'had a very exciting time' and happy that he 'would not have been away for worlds'.

The entrance to the upper yard of Dublin Castle. The work of Post Office telegraphists, based in the building on the right, was vital to the government's response to the rebellion.

(Stephen Ferguson)

ALDBOROUGH HOUSE

Aldborough House, built in the closing years of the eighteenth century as a town residence for Lord Aldborough, served in later years both as a progressive school[1] and as a military barracks before becoming, soon after the Crimean War, the principal depot of the Post Office Stores Branch. This imposing building in Portland Row remained until relatively recently an Aladdin's cave of Post Office materials from postage stamps to telegraph cables. On Easter Monday 1916, it fell to J. H. Reeves, Clerk (First Class) in the Stores Department, to ensure the safety of the building and the supply of telegraphic and engineering materials necessary to keep government and military communications open.

Reeves, who had joined the Post Office as a telegraphist in 1892, wrote a report of his actions during the Rising and this account provides another fascinating eyewitness record of events in that locality. He had seen active service in the army during the Boer War in South Africa and it is clear that he rather enjoyed the excitement of his undoubtedly dangerous position. His account is all the more vivid for this with additional manuscript comments added in the margins to supplement his typewritten report.

He was at home in Sutton on Monday afternoon when he was sent word that:

> the GPO and other Government buildings were in possession of the Sinn Feiners and that there was a riot in town.[2]

---

1 The Feinaglian Institution, established by Professor von Feinagle of Luxembourg.
2 BPMA Post 31/80.

Aldborough House as it was a few years before the Rising.

(Georgian Society Records)

He headed into town immediately and was lucky to catch a special Easter Excursion train at 3 p.m. At Aldborough House he met Mr Doak, Sectional Engineer, who confirmed the news that:

> the Post Office was being wrecked ... wires were cut and tramway and train services stopped.

Doak told him that he had been able to make contact with England from the telegraph office in Amiens Street and together they telegraphed to Sir William Slingo[3] to whom Reeves gave a synopsis of the engineering supplies – Wheatstone Apparatus, flame-proof wire, aerial cables and so forth – which he had in Aldborough House.

---

3   Engineer-in-Chief, Post Office Engineering Department, London.

Reeves, having told Doak that he would make sure he got whatever supplies he needed from the stores, concluded that he needed military protection for Aldborough House if the supplies there, and hence the communications line with England, were to be safeguarded. He made his way to the Post Office Parcels Office in Amiens Street, the railway station being at that time 'in a state of siege' and telephoned the Garrison Adjutant at Dublin Castle to ask for military protection. This was agreed and, leaving a few Stores Branch staff on duty in Aldborough House, he decided to try to get home by bicycle.

His journey was uneventful at first, but shortly after 6 p.m., when he was about a mile from Aldborough House, he came across a skirmish between the military and 'a patrol of Sinn Feiners'. He recalls:

> one young gentleman pointed his rifle at me but when I bellowed at him 'Don't shoot me: you'll get into awful trouble!' he lowered his rifle and told me to turn back.[4]

Having delivered this almost light-hearted scolding to the young Volunteer, Reeves could do nothing but return to the Stores Depot, where he watched from his ground-floor room as parties of armed Volunteers escorted 'wagon loads of ammunition and supplies to various pre-appointed destinations'. He had had the gates locked and given instructions that no lights were to be seen, so the presence of the few staff in the building seems to have passed unobserved by the Volunteers on the street. Without these precautions, it might well have occurred to the Volunteers to take possession of such an obvious strong point. Having checked again on the requirements of Mr Doak in Amiens Street, Reeves

---

4   BPMA Post 31/80.

eventually made his way home to Sutton after 10.15 p.m. On his way, he passed through two lines of Volunteer outposts with, as he says, 'the aid of a Dublin accent and a certain amount of "old-soldier sense"!'

The next day he was back in work early but, by this stage, the seriousness of the rebellion was becoming more apparent and Reeves was faced with staff deputations asking him to shut down. The engineering clerical staff, not under his control, left the building en bloc and, while he let it be known that he hoped staff would stay, he agreed that the ladies and any men who were particularly nervous or had a long way to go may leave. There was still no sign of the promised military guard, so he approached the officer who appeared to be in charge of operations at Amiens Street railway station to ask for an escort for the engineering supplies to be sent over to Doak. The officer, a Major Carter, said he couldn't do much for him as the sniping was intensifying, but Reeves managed to get the stores delivered by his own men. After this he tried to make his way home but was stopped at Annesley Bridge by the Volunteers who were 'by no means so polite as on the previous evening' and he had to return to Aldborough House and spend the night there.

On Wednesday morning the fighting was not so severe as to prevent him from going out to have his foot cauterised – it had been hurt somehow a few days earlier – and even getting home by bicycle for a few hours. However, he was back early in the afternoon and relieved to see that the promised military guard of about 100 soldiers – 4th Royal Dublin Fusiliers and Royal Irish Rifles – had arrived and had taken up positions on the roof of Aldborough House to fire against the Volunteer snipers. The arrival of the troops provoked more intense fighting and for the few Post Office staff who had chosen to stay or been unable to get home, the experience of 'sniping and collected fire' must have been very frightening. Sleep was impossible during the night and Reeves, with the assistance of E.W. Mann, a porter of whose bravery and devotion to duty he speaks highly, did his best to look after the remaining staff and military officers. By Thursday the situation was worse, with no possibility of communication with Amiens Street. 'If one walked from the hall-door to the gate at about 12 noon,' he recounts, 'one stood an excellent chance of being sniped.' For those staff eager to get home Reeves made out passes which he got signed by the military officers 'and left it to themselves to venture out of the building'. None of them, however, took the risk.

The shooting during that Thursday afternoon was particularly fierce and when a small body of Lancers replaced the Dublin Fusiliers, Reeves felt that the upper hand passed to those outside the building's walls. Having pointed out the positions of Volunteer snipers to an officer and corporal of the Lancers, he was on his way downstairs to help a wounded soldier when the officer 'came out of the room in a frightful state of distress to say that the corporal was shot dead'. Their position seems to have been very grave for a time, so much so that Lieutenant Davis of the Lancers wrote an urgent despatch for reinforcements. Since, however, 'no single man in khaki could at that time have got to Amiens Street', Reeves suggested a method which 'strictly speaking was a questionable subterfuge'. A corporation ambulance, which had called to take away the unfortunate corporal, was asked to deliver the despatch and after a very anxious half hour or so the reinforcements arrived. About 100 men 'doubled into the Depot and took shelter' with, he dryly remarks, 'an alacrity that one does not usually see at Territorial manoeuvres'.

With the arrival of the reinforcements Reeves, who was naturally anxious about the circumstances of his own family, decided to take advantage of what he thought was a falling off in the level of shooting outside in order to get home. He set off after 6 p.m. to walk, 'with a very cheap right foot', the six miles out to Sutton and was shot at for a distance of forty yards as far as Seville Place where a sentry looked at his pass from the shelter of a doorway and let him go on. He was also allowed through at the canal bridge but was stopped at Newcomen Bridge.[5] He then headed back to the canal but reported that he was stopped this time and so found himself caught between two military posts unable either to get home or return to Aldborough House. He noticed, 'by what I can say was only a special mercy of Providence', a side street, Nottingham Street, where he remembered one of his staff lived and turned into it. Sniping there was 'particularly brisk' drawing, he estimated, the fire from the soldiers on the GNR railway line at the end of the street. He knocked at door after door but had them banged in his face 'as the people were in a state of terror' until at last Mrs Brown, wife of a 3rd Class Storeman, took him in and put him up in the parlour for the night.[6] It was a night of 'incessant sniping', but in the morning he at last managed to get home to find his wife 'in a state of collapse' particularly on account of a 'foolish rumour … to the effect that Aldborough House had been burned down'.

At home over the weekend, Reeves only ventured out for food for his household and his attempts to get into the city on both Monday and Tuesday were unsuccessful. By that stage, the military cordon around the city centre was very tight. He did reach Aldborough House on Wednesday by writing out an official pass for himself. In a note in the margin of his report he confesses that

---

5   This may be a lapse. Annesley Bridge would seem to make more sense.
6   H. J. Brown of 37 Nottingham Street. He was subsequently officially thanked for his hospitality.

POST OFFICE STORES DEPARTMENT,
ALDBOROUGH HOUSE DEPÔT,
DUBLIN.

The bearer is Mr. J H Reeves Controller of Post Office Engineering Knies Ireland

J.H. Reeves
Briarfield
Sutton
3 May 1916

The pass written out for himself by J. H. Reeves of the Stores Branch.
(Courtesy of the BPMA)

on this and other occasions during the week he had felt obliged 'to assume myself a much higher official than what I am'. This had been particularly necessary when he had been in touch with the Garrison Adjutant. His self-appointed promotion, however, caused no ripples in the Post Office hierarchy in the circumstances and there is on the file, in fact, a red manuscript annotation added by the Controller of Stores in London, which states simply 'I agree that all's fair in love and war'.[7]

Reflecting on his experiences, Reeves concluded that his first consideration was to do everything to ensure the safety of the

---

7   BPMA Post 31/80.

building, not just from the rebels, but from the looters whose activities during the Rising drew unfavourable comment from participants on both sides of the conflict. He had no time for the 'virulent tribe of looters that were sacking the city unmolested, a really serious menace – more serious, according to many eye-witnesses, than the actual fighting'. Having secured Aldborough House, what comes through is the almost boyish delight he felt in the belief that he and his Stores Branch staff had done their bit during a crisis. 'It is a great thing,' he concludes, 'for our Department to have it to say that we carried on Post Office business as long as there was business at all to be done.'[8]

8   *Ibid.*

KINGSBRIDGE AND BEYOND

While the focus of Post Office attention was on critical sites like Crown Alley, Amiens Street and Dublin Castle, there was plenty of activity going on elsewhere and the response of GPO staff throughout the country was praiseworthy. Staff at Kingsbridge (now Heuston) station, for instance, where like Amiens Street there was a postal telegraph office, came under attack on several occasions during the week. In his report, W. J. Heaney, the overseer, records that on 26 April:

> Kingsbridge was under rebel fire from 3.55 p.m. to 5.10 p.m. The military authorities instructed staff to 'get under cover … No man to stand about the office'.[1]

Heaney goes on to note with a hint of pride that Sir Neville Chamberlain, Inspector-General of the RIC, 'was constantly in and out of the office, and on one occasion addressed the staff and said "You gentlemen are rendering invaluable service to the State".' It took another day before the doors and windows on the street side of the office were barricaded and protected by the erection of half-inch steel plates. Despite the obvious dangers of their position, Heaney was impressed with the loyalty and diligence of his staff: 'They were several times turned back when going off duty and were compelled to return to the office, and at other times were unable to reach the office.' This was despite their possession of official military passes, but as the week wore on, the cordon around the city grew ever tighter.

There had been one curious incident picked up at Kingsbridge

---

1   BPMA Post 31/80B.

early in the week which suggested that, for a little while, those who had taken over the GPO were able to use the communications system to their own advantage. A note on the files states that early on Tuesday 25 April, Heaney, at the Kingsbridge telegraph office, observed that the GPO called up Portarlington on the 'Dn-Portarlington Rail wire and asked "How many military have passed through Portarlington".[2] Heaney reports that he 'was astonished to hear Dublin calling and stopped the circuit'. He then spoke to the Portarlington operator, instructing him to give no information to Dublin until he had himself checked the identity of the caller in the GPO. Heaney called Dublin and asked, 'Who are you?' The reply 'Superintendent' was evasive and Heaney asked for a name. 'Dagg' came the reply, but when Heaney asked for more information on how he had got into the Instrument Room, he did not receive a reply. Convinced by now that he had been in contact with one of the Volunteers in the GPO, he instructed Portarlington to switch to another wire and to work directly through him in future. This little incident may well explain a statement in Norway's first report to Sir Evelyn Murray in London that Edward Gomersall, the Superintending Engineer, had managed 'to assure himself that the rebels in the GPO have no telegraphic comm. with other parts of Ireland'.[3]

Writing to the Engineer-in-Chief in London on 9 May, Gomersall was keen to put on record the bravery and devotion of his staff. In addition to the great work done by some of the senior men in his department whose efforts were crucial in restoring cross-channel and government communications, he picks out several particular instances of initiative. A senior inspector, Mr

2   BPMA Post 31/80B.
3   BPMA Post 56/177.

J. Winter, travelled from Amiens Street to Lucan by side-car on the night the rebellion broke out and did sterling work in redirecting trunk telegraph lines via other junctions. J. H. Shaw, an executive engineer who was on leave in Belfast, organised 'a special train and brought men down the Great Northern Line to Dublin, making good as he came'. Mr J. Jones, an inspector, saw the need to undertake work at Broadstone station and made his way there, passing through both military and rebel lines but, on his return journey, was taken prisoner by the rebels and searched:

> His passes were taken from him, but he was finally allowed to go under the threat of being shot if he disclosed the loss of his passes or if a rebel were caught with the passes in his possession.[4]

Belfast and the north of the country remained entirely quiet, but much of the work which would have been overseen in Dublin, both government telegraph traffic and cash remittance work, was handled through Belfast. By Tuesday of Easter week the temporary telegraph office at Amiens Street was receiving military telegrams, in cipher, from Belfast but, since the normal northern wires had been systematically cut, the messages had to be routed through the Central Telegraph Office in London.[5] Normal mailboat despatches on the Larne–Stranraer, Belfast–Fleetwood and Belfast–Heysham routes were temporarily suspended by military order and censorship restrictions applied initially on all telegraph traffic. Despite this the Belfast postmaster, S. G. Forsythe, did make arrangements for some mails to be sent via Liverpool. It is clear from his report of 4 May that he was taking no chances in relation to potential disloyalty amongst the staff in his district:

---

4   BPMA Post 31/80B.
5   BPMA Post 56/177.

Having been informed confidentially by the Commissioner of Police that two officers employed at Clandeboye and Shane's Park Military Camp Post Offices, though not Sinn Feiners, held such strong political views as to render their employment in such posts undesirable in view of the gravity of the crisis, I thought it necessary to recall them and replace them by men whose loyalty was above suspicion.[6]

While the spirit of the rebellion of 1798 had been well extinguished in the north of the country, the embers still burned in County Wexford. There was a small outbreak in Enniscorthy, under Robert Brennan, when the town was occupied and some trouble too in Ferns but, thanks in large part to the good sense of the local military commander who was a Wexford man, bloodshed was avoided. There are on file, however, some interesting remarks from the postmaster of New Ross, J. J. Webb, who highlights the tension that had arisen in the county over recruitment to the army and the consequences this might have had for the post office in the town:

> The police having obtained detailed copies of the plans on one of the 46 Sinn Feiners since arrested here, it is now known that the rebels had contemplated taking the town, the Post Office being the first place to be taken at all risks. It is also beyond doubt that had they occupied New Ross this office would have been completely destroyed … as a resentment to 72% of the eligible men in my district having joined the Army – every eligible man at the Head Office having joined, particularly as one of my postmen (now a Recruiting Sergeant here) has been instrumental in obtaining some hundreds of recruits to the Army.[7]

6   BPMA Post 31/80B.
7   *Ibid.*, Report of 10 May 1916.

A number of Wexford staff were implicated in the Rising and arrested, but most were subsequently reinstated.

MISCONDUCT.

Officer _Mr. John o'Neill_   Rank _S.C. &_

DATE.	NATURE OF IRREGULARITY.	PUNISHMENT, AND BY WHOM AUTHORISED.
Apl 1916	Suspended from duty in connection with Sinn Fein disturbances: reinstated on recommendation of Fleetwood Wilson-Byrne Committee.	P.M.G. 2.9.1916

Suspected of involvement in the rebellion, this County Wexford telegraphist was suspended but later reinstated in line with the recommendations of the Wilson-Byrne commission.

(An Post archives)

Blackened pots and pans in the GPO kitchen where food was prepared for the garrison during Easter week.

(Courtesy of the BPMA)

Rebels in the Ranks – Joining the Rising

While the vast majority of Post Office staff played no part in the Rising and would, both by temperament and by virtue of their status as civil servants, have been reluctant to express any strong political opinions at all, there were a few whose interests went beyond sporting and cultural enthusiasm to active involvement in nationalist politics and militant action. Some of these people, as has been seen, came under suspicion before the Rising took place and, in so far as he felt it necessary, Norway took action against them. Others managed to avoid any official scrutiny until their involvement became plain after the Rising began.

The Wilson-Byrne Inquiry considered the cases of Irish civil servants implicated in the Rising and at the top of the Post Office section of that list was Richard Mulcahy who, as soldier and politician, would go on to play a prominent part in Irish life until his retirement in 1961. Dick Mulcahy came from a Post Office family, with his father, who had started as a clerk in Waterford, ending up as postmaster of Ennis. His younger brother, Paddy, joined the Department but, like many other members of staff, left to join up in 1915. Paddy survived the war, returned to his job in the Post Office, from which he was subsequently dismissed for involvement with local republicans, and had a very successful career in the Irish army.

Dick joined the Post Office in 1902 and worked in various parts of the country until his transfer to Dublin in 1907. There he attended technical college and trained for the Post Office engineering diploma. Attached to the engineering branch and based in Aldborough House, where he might well have known

J. H. Reeves, it fell to him to cut the telegraph and telephone wires that ran alongside the Great Northern Railway line to Belfast. (Reeves, of course, was his Stores Branch colleague who ensured that the necessary supplies were available to patch them together again!) Having cut the wires, Mulcahy went on to join Thomas Ashe in the successful attack on the RIC barracks at Ashbourne. His case presented no ambiguity to the Wilson-Byrne inquiry and he duly ended up in Frongoch as a prisoner. Dick Mulcahy's involvement in the Irish Volunteers was known to his father, the postmaster, who did not approve and frequently reminded his family that he was himself 'a servant of the British Government and had done well by them.'[1] Dick's younger sister, Kitty, recalls that 'Easter 1916 stunned Papa but when at last he got a letter from Dick from Frongoch … he took it calmly and with much relief'.

It is no surprise that other Post Office Engineering Branch staff also feature prominently in the Wilson-Byrne list. These, after all, were the men who knew the lay-out of the telegraph and telephone cable network in the city and along the main railway lines, and their knowledge was vital to the rebel plans to disrupt and delay as much as possible the government's response to the Rising. Another Post Office man, Seán Byrne, recalled that on the Wednesday of Holy Week a few of the engineering staff attended a meeting chaired by Dermot Lynch, who told them that 'a special squad was being formed' which would cut communications 'so as to isolate the city'.[2] The following night they met again, this time with Thomas MacDonagh presiding, and the jobs were shared out

1   Risteárd Mulcahy, *Richard Mulcahy (1886–1971) a Family Memoir*, p. 10.
2   BMH WS 0579. Dermot Lynch was a member of the Supreme Council of the IRB and had started his career as a Boy Clerk in Cork post office.

– Andy Fitzpatrick was to cut the cross channel cable from the
GPO at a point in Talbot Street, James Tyrell was to do similar
work at Dun Laoghaire, John Twamley at Shankill and the Citizen
Army brothers, Martin and George King, were to cut the cables
in Westland Row. Byrne himself was charged with cutting down
the pole and wire carrying the western trunks at Broom Bridge
level crossing in Cabra. On Good Friday morning Fitzpatrick
and Martin King took a stroll around the city centre noting
manholes and junctions of particular importance, places like the
Lombard Street corner which carried a special direct wire between
Dublin Castle and London, and the Palace Street junction which
contained a host of police wires.

John Twamley, in the statement he gave to the Bureau of
Military Archives in December 1951, describes the confusion
and uncertainty caused by the cancellation of the Easter Sunday
arrangements and the steps he had to take to check the position
on Monday morning. Once he had clarified with Dermot Lynch
that the Rising was on, he went to Bray, where he was based, and
made his way over the fields to the railway line where he 'climbed
the poles and cut the telephone and telegraph wires and all the
railway signal wires'.[3] This done, he returned to the main road and
cut the Bray–Shankill wire. With a short stop for refreshment at
the Lamb Doyle's in the Dublin foothills, he made his way back
to town. There was a rope across the road at Portobello Barracks
on the Rathmines Road, the first sign he had that the rebellion
had started, and as he mingled in the crowd he noticed blood on
the back of an officer's uniform. Twamley found another route into
town and reported to the GPO. At the end of the week, as the
Post Office was engulfed in flames, he was one of a small group

3   BMH WS 0629.

that broke into a house on the corner of Moore Street and Henry Place. There, he remembers:

> I was confronted by an old man and woman who were frightened out of their wits. I told them they would be quite safe but they would not stay with us. Instead they locked themselves in the basement.[4]

In those few words is a reminder, if one is needed, that amongst the plans and politics, the deeds and daring of the Rising, it was the ordinary people of Dublin who suffered most in the course of the insurrection.

Maurice Collins, a Sorting Clerk & Telegraphist in the GPO, joined the IRB in 1908 or 1909. During the Rising he was based at a house on the corner of North King Street and subsequently in the Four Courts. During the week he had taken prisoner a Castle detective and given specific instructions that he was to be well treated. His statement recalled how, at Richmond Barracks, as many of his comrades were 'picked out for court-martial or deportation by members of the G Division' the detective whom he had kept prisoner 'passed me by although he knew me well', a living example, perhaps, of the old tale of Androcles and the Lion.[5]

Collins spent time in Frongoch but was freed in July on the decision of the Sankey committee which reviewed the cases of interned prisoners. Notwithstanding his release, the Wilson-Byrne inquiry recommended his dismissal from the Post Office, a decision questioned in the House of Commons by P. J. O'Shaughnessy, MP for Limerick West. Replying, Sir Herbert Samuel, Home Secretary, made the point that 'it by no means follows that because … a person need not be kept any longer in detention he

---

4   *Ibid.*
5   BMH WS 0550.

is, therefore, suitable to be reinstated in the Civil Service of the Crown.'[6] Though dismissed from his position in the Post Office, Collins seems to have benefitted from what may have been an administrative oversight, in that he continued to be paid his salary up until Christmas. With the proceeds he opened a shop in Parnell Street which subsequently became an important link in Michael Collins' system for intercepting government letters.

The façade of the GPO – scarred but still dignified.
(Courtesy of the National Library of Ireland. Alb. 107)

6   *Hansard*, 19 October 1916.

Picking up the Pieces

Norway had been under pressure from the Lord Lieutenant, Lord Wimborne and the Under Secretary to reintroduce some sort of postal service in Dublin during Easter week itself. He quite rightly felt that the situation was far too dangerous for this and observed that 'the appearance of a Mail Car or any person in official uniform on the streets would … have been simply madness'. With access to the city virtually impossible and sniping 'almost universal', his view seems quite reasonable, but he notes that it was accepted by his political superiors 'somewhat reluctantly'.[1] Conscious that some sort of official enquiry into their stewardship would inevitably follow the suppression of the rebellion, they were probably keen to play down the significance of events in Dublin by demonstrating a swift return to normality.

The Post Office did manage to despatch a small mail to England on the evening of 29 April, but Norway, writing to Murray in London on 30 April, made it quite clear that he was not prepared to take responsibility for ordering the resumption of services 'unless and until the military authorities give me clear assurances of the reasonable – not absolute – safety of my staff'. Enough dangers, he felt, had been risked already by 'those whose obligations were for the moment of essential importance to the public safety', but he was not prepared to call on his staff 'to risk their lives merely to get a little correspondence into England a day or two sooner'.[2]

When the fighting was over, the extent of the destruction became apparent and it was clear that the GPO, so recently gleaming from

---

1   BPMA Post 31/80.
2   BPMA Post 56/177.

its renovation, would be useless from any operational aspect. With commendable speed, however, a temporary sorting office was established within the Rotunda buildings, part of which was at that time an ice rink, and sorting and delivery work had begun again by the morning of 3 May. Mrs Norway was highly impressed with the industry of the staff – 'a regular hive of bees' – busy sorting with no proper fittings but what they 'had contrived for themselves out of seats, benches and old scenery'.[3] Just three days after the end of hostilities, the whole postal service had been reorganised and two daily deliveries reinstated in Dublin.

The temporary GPO Sorting Office set up in the Rotunda on 3 May 1916: note the benches set on top of each other to aid sorting.

(Courtesy of the BPMA)

The telegraph work, which had been maintained so conscientiously by Post Office staff throughout the Rising, was put on a proper footing with the top floor of the Parcels' Office in Amiens Street being converted into an Instrument Room. Military restrictions remained on public access to the system, but the Post Office

3   Mrs Hamilton Norway, *The Sinn Fein Rebellion as I saw it*, p. 87.

The North American section of the temporary Sorting Office.

(Courtesy of the BPMA)

engineering staff had the new office ready for business by 9 May. In a hint that dealing with the army was not always plain sailing, Norway comments that 'the varying requirements of the Military in respect of Telegraph and Telephone restrictions were very disturbing and caused infinite trouble'.[4]

The military authorities, however, must have been generally pleased with the efforts made by Norway's officials on their behalf. In relation to the arrangements made to ensure payment of separation allowances to the wives of soldiers at the Front – an issue of particular importance to the army command – and old age pensions, they wrote an appreciative letter to him. Since the relevant records had been destroyed in the GPO, the Department had had to draw on details held elsewhere in order to prepare the payments. Norway requested an armoured car to accompany the staff who were to distribute the funds to the various branch and sub-offices in Dublin, and his wife records the excitement when

4   BPMA Post 31/80.

May 1916 – Waiting for old age and separation payments to be made at Aungier Street post office.

(Courtesy of the BPMA)

one of those home-made 'monsters' with a reinforced engine boiler mounted on a lorry chassis turned up outside the Royal Hibernian Hotel before proceeding to the Bank of Ireland to collect £10,000 in silver for delivery throughout the city.

While the GPO was the headquarters of many Post Office staff, the Department held several other buildings in the city, including a number in the Sackville Street area. The Accountant's Office, on the opposite side of the street from the GPO, had escaped the worst of the destruction but fell victim to the fires started on the night the insurrection ended. Writing to Murray in his report of 30 April, Norway observed that:

> The blaze was such that the Fire Brigade – which was out as shooting had ceased at that spot – could do nothing. I appealed to Nathan to

compel them with Military aid to attempt to save the Accountant's Office: but he assured me nothing could be done.[5]

Speculation on the future of the GPO itself was widespread with rumours that the shell was to be pulled down. One suggestion put forward by the President of the Royal Institute of the Architects of Ireland, Mr R. Caulfield Orpen, who was perhaps rather optimistically thinking ahead to the introduction of Home Rule, was that a new House of Parliament should be built on the GPO site. This, he thought, would appeal particularly to Ulstermen whose:

> first view on leaving Amiens Street Station is of the House of Parliament beckoning to them from up a beautiful avenue to send their members to take their rightful share in the government of the country they love.[6]

The Secretary's registry in the GPO. Years of Post Office records were reduced to the ash which covers the floor.

(Courtesy of the BPMA)

---

5   BPMA Post 56/177.

6   See *The Irish Builder*, Vol. 58, No. 15.

The Henry Street corner of the ruined GPO. The small tent covers access to the cable chamber underneath.

(Courtesy of the BPMA)

Few people can have imagined then that thirteen years would pass before the rebuilding of the GPO would be completed.

The GPO continued to smoulder for several days after the end of the fighting, but as soon as possible the debris was carefully examined to see if anything could be salvaged from the wreckage. Very little was left, with Post Office records and ledgers reduced to 'a mound of what looked like solid white chalk' which, Mrs Norway records, 'felt like silk between my fingers'. Watching the workmen sift through the wreckage in her husband's office, she

The GPO Parcels' Office in Amiens Street. The top floor was converted into a telegraph office after the destruction of the GPO.

(Stephen Ferguson)

was reminded of the excavations at Pompeii and delighted when, amongst the ruins, three little brooches given to her by her son 'when a wee boy' were recovered.[7]

Elsewhere in the wreckage, money to the value of £185 was found and deposited in the Savings Bank. The Accountant General proposed to credit the Appropriation-in-Aid account if it remained unclaimed at the end of the year.[8] He recommended a similar course in respect of the £149 10s. found on one of the prisoners arrested at the GPO. Official cash lost in the GPO during the Rising was estimated at £2,792 18s. 7d. and would be charged to the Default Vote in the Government Estimates.[9] Parcels and registered letters

7   Mrs Hamilton Norway, *The Sinn Fein Rebellion as I saw it*, pp. 94, 96.
8   Sir Charles King, Comptroller and Accountant General, London.
9   This was a government budget class to account for unexpected expenditure or losses like this.

9 May 1916 – telegraph staff start work in the new Instrument Room in
the Amiens Street Parcels' Office.

(Courtesy of the National Library of Ireland. Alb. 107.)

were destroyed, of course, and the question of compensation of
customers arose. The solicitor's advice at the time was, however,
unambiguously in favour of the Post Office:

> A common carrier who takes proper care is not liable to the owner of
> goods conveyed by him for loss occasioned by 'the act of God or the
> King's enemies'.[10]

---

10 BPMA Post 31/80.

Recrimination and Commendation

Throughout his reports, Norway is keenly appreciative of the efforts made and dangers faced by his staff in keeping communications open. While he had made a point of distributing commendations himself, he suggested to Sir Evelyn Murray 'the expediency of coming over personally for a day or so' as a way of recognising just how much the Department owed to postal staff. 'A big thing has happened here, to which I know no parallel', he continues, and a commendation 'from you … would be very highly appreciated'.[1] Staff were shocked by the events that had occurred in their midst and were quick to dissociate themselves from the Rising. One important union, the Association of Irish Post Office Clerks, which had lost its premises and records in Henry Street, issued an editorial repudiation in relation to the 'dire disaster in Easter week', taking particular umbrage at the 'unfounded assertion' put forward in certain sections of the press 'cross-channel and Irish … that the Post Office in Dublin was "a nest of Sinn Feiners".' The only reason the editor could find for this exercise of 'journalistic imaginations' was the fact that the GPO was the first building attacked and that the staff on duty had left the premises 'at the point of the bayonet and amidst the whizzing of bullets'. He went on to emphasise that the staff knew well the Department's prohibition on active participation in political movements and concluded that 'of 369 S.C.&T.s in the Dublin Sorting Office' there were question marks over just five people,

---

1   BPMA Post 156/177. Both the Secretary, Sir Evelyn Murray, and the Assistant Postmaster General, Herbert Pease MP, did visit Dublin after the Rising.

while of the 'nearly 400 in the Telegraph Office' only two were arrested.[2]

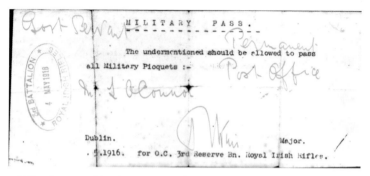

Official permits like this were issued to some GPO staff to allow them to pass through military checkpoints.

(An Post archives)

For Chief Secretary Birrell the Rising was a personal disaster from which his career never recovered. He resigned immediately after its suppression and was held by the Hardinge Commission to be largely accountable for allowing it to happen. Wimborne and Nathan also subsequently resigned, although Wimborne was reappointed as Lord Lieutenant later in the year. Other senior officials were also tarnished. Commenting on the GPO in his evidence to the Royal Commission on the Rebellion in Ireland, Nathan did express regret that 'there was not a strong guard on the Post Office'.[3] Norway, perhaps anticipating criticism here, had been astute enough to address this point early on in his first report to Murray on 27 April. Clearly, the outcome of Easter Monday's occupation of the GPO might have been different if

---

2   *The Irish Postal and Telegraph Guardian*, May–June 1916.
3   *Royal Commission on the Rebellion in Ireland: Minutes of Evidence*, p. 10.

the Instrument Room guard had had ammunition in their guns.
Norway's clear recollection of the instructions in August 1914 was
that 'each man of the guard should have his magazine charged, and
cut-off closed, and should fire to stop any unauthorized person'.
However:

> the soldiers had, at some subsequent time, without my knowledge,
> been deprived of cartridges and were accordingly powerless.[4]

Norway dealt at some length with the question of the loyalty of
Post Office staff when he was giving evidence before the Commission, stating that:

> ever since I have been in Dublin I have heard it said from time to
> time that the Post Office was full of Sinn Feiners. As often as that
> statement was made I have called for evidence in support of it, and
> never got it.[5]

He acknowledged a number of clear cases where he had taken
disciplinary action against staff known to be disloyal. In assessing
allegations of disloyalty, however, Norway went out of his way to
admit only compelling evidence. He told the Commission that:

> Throughout this whole matter (the) Postmaster-General had consid-
> ered himself not only as the guardian of the public safety but, to some
> extent, also as protector of the postal staff against possible injustice.[6]

A list of forty-six people against whom there was some suspicion
was compiled but, in the context of 17,000 employees, Norway can
have felt no hesitation in robustly defending the loyalty of his staff.

---

4   BPMA Post 56/177.

5   *Royal Commission on the Rebellion in Ireland: Minutes of Evidence,* p. 63.

6   *Ibid.*, pp. 62–3.

In a speech to the House of Commons on 31 July 1916, Major Walter Guinness alleged that a GPO clerk had telephoned on 25 April to the Cork operator with the message 'Dublin has risen: let Cork rise'. Norway dismissed this and wrote to Murray, the Secretary in London, on 16 August delicately suggesting that:

> the Postmaster General may desire to afford Major Guinness an opportunity of publicly withdrawing the charge, as an honourable gentleman should, unless he can substantiate it.[7]

Two members of the Stores Branch staff were transferred from Dublin to the Stafford detention barracks on 30 April. Mr W. S. Doherty (Assistant Clerk) was able to give a satisfactory account of his movements and was released, but another employee, Mr M. Cremen (3rd Class Clerk), was warned that 'unless he ceased all connection with the Irish Volunteers, the Postmaster General would have no alternative but to dismiss him from his appointment in the Post Office without further warning'. He duly gave an undertaking to sever his links with the Volunteers and was allowed to return to duty.

For the great majority of Post Office staff, the Rising must have come as a shock and an unnecessary and dangerous disruption to their lives. For those few whose senior position or rostering on the day meant that they were necessarily caught up in the turmoil of Easter week, Norway had nothing but praise: 'the spirit in which great difficulties were met and overcome was one of conspicuous loyalty and devotion'.[8] The question of how this loyalty might be rewarded was the subject of some correspondence between Dublin and London. Writing to Norway on 21 June, Murray mentions the

7   BPMA Post 31/80B.
8   BPMA Post 31/80B.

case of E. W. Mann, the porter who had been so helpful to Reeves in Aldborough House:

> I don't much like the idea of distributing largesse among the P.O. staff and I don't know where the line is to be drawn. How would a grant of £5 affect the position of the Engineering and Telephone staff?

Norway's natural inclination lay on the side of caution and restraint, even in these most unusual circumstances, and he was not keen to recommend any additional payments to staff 'other of course than extra duty pay actually earned'. He was also very conscious of the need to be fair and replying to Murray admitted Mann's good conduct, but went on to say that 'many of the staff in Dublin ran equal risk to life during the insurrection, and some incurred definitely more'. Those actually on duty during the insurrection should, he felt, be given extra leave as a mark of appreciation of unusually trying work done in circumstances of some personal danger, but 'I should be sorry, on full reflection, to go further' he concluded. In his report to London, he also placed on record the 'quite exceptional exertions' made by his senior staff – Gomersall (Superintending Engineer), H. J. Tipping (Controller Dublin Postal Service), Kenny (Controller of Telegraphs) and Reeves (Stores Branch) – in restoring service after the Rising. The postmasters of Belfast, Cork and Kingstown, and Mr Coonan, his senior Principal Clerk, who 'came to me at my hotel on each day of the insurrection often at much personal risk', were also particularly mentioned by Norway in his report.

The vital and obvious importance of the work done by staff on the engineering and telegraph side should not detract from the efforts of staff in other areas. Within the greater Dublin Postal District – in Portobello, Rathgar and Fairview delivery offices for instance – there were several who received commendations. In fact, Tipping, the Controller, doing his best to be fair divided his staff into three classes:

– officers considered 'to have run some risk'
– officers who 'rendered useful service but didn't run serious risk'
– officers who merely 'acted with commendable zeal'.

Not all indeed felt that their services had been adequately recognised. Michael Patchell, an Assistant Inspector of Postmen, rescued the keys of some 1400 Dublin and suburban collection boxes from the ruins of the GPO and, by filing away the molten glass and brass that had stuck between the wards of the keys, enabled collections to resume within thirty-six hours. In an elaborate memorial he petitioned the Postmaster General for more than the 'highly commended' on his service record, but nothing more was done. A civilian, Mr R. Best of Sutton, claimed that it was his prompt action in alerting Reeves of the Stores Branch to the occupation of the GPO that really saved the telegraph connections between Dublin and London. In reply the Post Office thanked him but indicated that the matter had already been taken in hand.

Retribution for the leaders of the Rising was swift and those who signed the Proclamation cannot have expected to escape execution although the idea, which emerged many years later, that an instruction from Asquith, the Prime Minister, ordering postponement of Connolly's execution was overturned because General Maxwell threatened to resign is fascinating in its suggestion of an alternative outcome. Maxwell, certainly, was diligent in rounding up and detaining a great many more people than actually took part in the rebellion. The Sankey committee, set up to review the cases of people interned in England after the Rising, advised the government on their continued detention in

The ruins of the GPO's main Sorting Office.

(Courtesy of the National Library of Ireland. Alb. 107.)

The GPO loading yard looking towards Nelson's Pillar.

(Courtesy of the National Library of Ireland. Alb. 107.)

the context of the Defence of the Realm Regulations. The Home Secretary, Sir Herbert Samuel, however, established another body at the end of July 1916 to establish the degree of involvement of Post Office and other Irish civil servants in the Rising. This arose in response to concerns that implicated officials might be condemned on the basis of military evidence alone. Sir Guy Fleetwood Wilson, a distinguished colonial civil servant, and Sir William Byrne, a former Irish Under Secretary, were appointed to conduct a review of the cases and their report contains interesting insights into the alleged involvement of some Post Office staff.[9] When, some thirty-five years later, some of these men chose to make statements to the Bureau of Military History on their role in the Rising, the extent of their actual involvement becomes clear.

The Wilson-Byrne committee did its work efficiently and took pains to do it sensitively and impartially. At the outset, it declined to take the office provided in Dublin Castle, on the grounds that this might prove rather intimidating to some of those called before it, and took rooms elsewhere instead. Wilson and Byrne saw themselves as civil servants interviewing fellow civil servants and sought to convey the message that 'it would be a genuine pleasure to us … should we find ourselves able to recommend their reinstatement'. Indeed, they adopted what some may have seen as an excessively lenient attitude in dealing with those whose cases they considered:

> Owing to the peculiar political situation in Ireland, we did not, broadly speaking, judge men only from the standpoint of their continued

---

9   Professor Keith Jeffery kindly drew my attention to the report of the Wilson-Byrne Inquiry, *Report on the cases of Irish civil servants suspended in connection with the recent rebellion*, and was the first to publish its findings. See *The GPO and the Easter Rising*, p. 188, where he attributes the creation of the committee to Norway's influence. As a former Postmaster General, Herbert Samuel would certainly have been acquainted with Norway.

connection with the Sinn Fein movement. We were guided by their activities, their explanation thereof, by their mental attitude towards the rebellion, and by their expressed intention in the future to subordinate or otherwise, their loyalty as public servants, to their political creed.[10]

Their approach, in the circumstances, was generous and of the forty-two people whom they interviewed, eighteen were recommended for reinstatement in their respective departments. Not surprisingly, given its size within the service, over half of those examined came from the Post Office, with eleven being allowed to return to their jobs. Since Wilson-Byrne confined itself only to those civil servants who were under suspension and took the view that those still in military detention were, *ipso facto*, unsuitable for reinstatement, the list of Post Office staff suspected of complicity in the rebellion is longer and contains forty-six names.[11]

Some civil servants listed in the Wilson-Byrne report claimed that they had been unwilling participants in the events of Easter week and had ended up being arrested because they had been taken prisoner by the rebels. One such was James Heery, a clerical assistant in the engineering branch, who left his lodgings in Fitzroy Avenue on the evening of Easter Monday and did not return. He was arrested after the Rising, taken to Richmond Barracks and deported and, on his release on 14 June, applied to take up his job again. This was not allowed for, in the meantime, a search of his rooms had revealed 'a quantity of Post Office stationery ... 1 rifle cartridge, 1 revolver cartridge' and an Irish Volunteers membership card. Heery, having been refused immediate reinstatement, offered the following explanation of his whereabouts on 24 April:

10 *Ibid.*, p. 191.
11 See Appendix 3 for the names.

The GPO Engine Room after the Rising.

(Courtesy of the BPMA)

At 11 a.m. I went for a walk along the Canal Bank, which I frequently do, to Lucan and returned about 4 p.m., when I had my dinner. I went out again about 5 p.m. and near Nelson's Pillar, was forced by two armed men into the General Post Office and was kept a prisoner by rebels until the surrender to the Military took place … it is clearly evident that I was entirely innocent of any connection directly or indirectly with the insurgent movement.[12]

He adds that Mrs Jauncey, 'who is a good loyalist', could verify the times of his coming and going. What she could not verify, of course, was his story of being taken prisoner at the Pillar and brought in to the GPO and, in respect of this and similar accounts, one detects in the report of Sir Guy Fleetwood-Wilson and Sir William Byrne a note of polite scepticism:

12 Keith Jeffery, *The GPO and the Easter Rising*, p. 214.

> In no instance were we altogether satisfied that such Civil Servants as
> actually took part in the rebellion, under alleged compulsion, could not
> have withdrawn at an early stage of it.[13]

In this case, Heery may well have given a false name when he was
arrested and on release there would have been nothing, beyond
suspicion, to tie him to the rebellion. More often than not, people
examined were quite ready to give an account of their political
views 'freely, frankly and unblushingly' and, much to the surprise
of the Wilson-Byrne committee, saw no inconsistency between
those views and their position as civil servants provided they
'discharged (their) official duties satisfactorily during office hours'.

The administrative procedure to be used for dismissing staff
gave rise to some discussion at the Irish Office. Writing to the
Attorney General on 9 September 1916, Sir Edward O'Farrell
wondered whether:

> we should leave the Post Office and the other English Departments
> concerned to dismiss their own men, or whether this should be done
> by His Excellency's order, as the men are serving in Ireland.[14]

Replying a couple of days later, the Attorney General advised that
the Lord Lieutenant should be responsible for dismissing all staff
implicated and goes on to express his support for the idea that 'for
the future all Civil Servants of the Crown should be requested to
take the oath of allegiance'. A difference of approach also emerged
on the question of pay. Irish civil servants outside the Post Office
were being paid up to the time of their dismissal and the Irish
Office sought to have the same policy applied in relation to Post

---

13 *Ibid.*, p. 191.
14 United Kingdom National Archives CO 904/25/1.

Office staff. The matter went, by way of parliamentary question, beyond Norway to London where Sir Evelyn Murray, the Secretary, maintained the Post Office point of view, writing in a letter of 8 November 1916 that the Postmaster General:

> hesitates to modify his decision that officers dismissed from the Post Office service for complicity in the rebellion should receive no Post Office pay subsequent to the date of suspension.[15]

In this ever so polite refusal, Murray diplomatically added that he naturally wished to cause no embarrassment to the Irish government.

15 *Ibid.*

LETTERS FROM THE FRONT

In his reports to London, Norway emphasises that he came under some pressure to restore a normal postal service before, in his view, it was safe to do so. The government, in the midst of the crisis, naturally looked to the Post Office and its public face, the friendly postman, as a symbol of reassurance and normality in a disordered and frightened city. There were practical implications too, of course, for the letter and postcard were still firmly fixed as the primary means of ordinary communication for most people and, in wartime especially, letters to and from Irish soldiers on the continent were the only way of keeping in touch with sons and husbands at war. Indeed, when the GPO was occupied on Easter Monday, a few British soldiers, perhaps home on leave, happened to be in the Public Office at the time. They, along with those who had been guarding the Instrument Room upstairs, were taken prisoner. The O'Rahilly, who was in charge of prisoners and whose conduct and attitude throughout the Rising drew favourable notice, undertook to have letters delivered to their wives who lived on the north side of the city. Min Ryan and another couple of women were instructed to deliver them. She recalled the circumstances many years later:

> Wednesday morning we started off to deliver those letters. We had been up all night. Our feet got very tired. It was terribly warm ... we went on out and delivered all the letters. I always remember the look on the women's faces when they read the messages. We asked: 'Is there any message?' They looked at us as if we were awful women.[1]

---

1   BMH WS 0399.

Thomas Cassin joined the Royal Dublin Fusiliers in August 1914 and survived the war to return to his job as postman in December 1918.

(An Post archives)

Letters to and from the Front were a great source of comfort in the midst of the First World War for Irishmen serving in the army and those written to Monica Roberts are a remarkable survival from that time. They bear witness to the suffering of those Irishmen who volunteered for service in the war and give an indication also of the general organisational efficiency of the Department which, in conjunction with the army's system, delivered letters and parcels to soldiers (and prisoners too) from Ypres and Limburg to the Dardanelles. They are also the medium for comments on how the Rising was perceived by men whose daily lives brought them face to face with death.

Monica Roberts, daughter of a clergyman and vice-Provost of Trinity College, lived in Stillorgan in County Dublin. Shortly after the start of the war, she set up a group which she called the Band of Helpers. It dedicated itself to providing small items of practical use and comfort for Irish soldiers – razors, cigarettes, books, socks and so forth – and Monica herself wrote many letters to men, predominantly soldiers of the Royal Dublin Fusiliers, in France. The letters she received were preserved by her daughter and presented to the Royal Dublin Fusiliers archive.[2] It is an extensive collection, running to nearly 400 items, and provides a unique insight into the lives of men in the trenches. Some are very literate, well composed and carefully written, others are a little more rough and ready, with Dublin expression and pronunciation clearly to the fore, but all, written in ink or scribbled in pencil on scraps of whatever paper was available, bear an honesty and immediacy that comes from men who know they may never write another letter.

---

2   For the background to this collection see Bryan MacMahon's article, *The Monica Roberts Collection of Letters from the Western Front, 1914–1918*, in *The Irish Sword*, Vol. XXVI, 2008.

Within the confines of military censorship, there are glimpses into the horror of that war, into its relentless and endless futility and the bravery and self-sacrifice of soldiers, as well as flashes of humour, memories of Dublin life and a yearning for romance. It was a remarkable undertaking for a young woman which called not just for a highly compassionate nature but a mature and robust character as well. It is impossible, even a century later, to be unaffected by the cheerful letter of 4 April 1916 from Private Patrick Byrne of John Street West, Dublin – 'you would never hear us Chaps grumble' – and to see beside it the envelope with the annotation 'KIA 20/4/16 Recommended for the V.C.' Maintaining an encouraging and genuine correspondence in such circumstances cannot have been easy.

The letters that regularly made their way to Monica's house, Kelston, in Stillorgan, generally arrived in official printed envelopes which bore the signed declaration of the soldier that 'the contents of this envelope refer to nothing but private and family matters'. They might still be opened for inspection by the army censorship staff, but most were allowed to pass on the basis of the personal certification given. Much that was not strictly of a 'private and family' nature did make its way to Monica Roberts but most of the correspondence deals with the daily concerns of the men – life in the trenches, battling with the 'Huns', expressions of gratitude for the parcels received and requests for particular items that would be appreciated. What is of particular interest, in the context of 1916, are the views expressed in these letters on the Rising for these are the opinions of men who believed they fought for Ireland and the freedom that would follow Home Rule every bit as much as they fought against Kaiser Bill.

The feeling of being let down by the rebels in Dublin, 'stabbed in the back' as the Irish Parliamentary Party MP and

Name	Post Office Rank	Office
Sec. Lieut. Coyne, J. J. A.	Clerk, 3rd Class	Stores Dept.
Sec. Lieut. Savage, H. G.	Sorter	L.P.S., N.W. District
Armstrong, C.	Postman	Readhead, Carlisle
Bagust, H. O.	Assistant Postman	L.P.S., E.C. District
Boys, T. H.	Postman	L.P.S., N. District
Breedon, W. C.	Postman	Portsmouth
Barley, H. E.	Postman	Bedford
Burns, J.	Boy Messenger	L.P.S., W. District
Burns, R.	Auxiliary Postman	Belfast
Collins, T. C.	Sorter	L.P.S., S.W. District
Cox, L. G.	Postman	Portsmouth
Currie, W.	Labourer	Engrg. Dept., N.E. District
Davies, W. B.	Assistant Clerk	Savings Bank Dept.
Donnelly, L.	Postman	Hull
Dowson, J. H.	Postman	Middlesbrough
Drummond, W. J.	Postman	Newcastle-on-Tyne
Dunne, J.	Postman	Warrington
Dunne, P. J.	Unestbd. Skilled Workman	Engrg. Dept., Ireland
Ewings, J. D.	Boy Messenger	Engrg. Dept., Met. Power Dist.
Eyres, E. F.	S.C. & T.	Salisbury
Faulkner, M.	Temporary Postman	Ashbourne
Fulford, W.	Labourer	Engrg. Dept., S. Mid. Dist.
Gillman, A. J. G.	Boy Messenger	L.P.S., N. District
Goodwin, H. M.	Postman	L.P.S., N.W. District
Griffiths, J. C.	Youth	Engrg. Dept., S. Lancs. Dist.
Griffiths, L. J.	Temporary Postman	Kington
Haley, E.	Auxiliary Postman	Curragh Camp
Hall, A.	Postman	Pershore, Worcester
Hall, M.	Postman	Gosport
Hall, R. H.	Tradesman	Engrg. Dept., S. Lancs. Dist.
Hammond, W. J.	Postman	Magherafelt, Belfast
Hicks, R.	Postman	Bolton
Hogan, M.	Auxiliary Postman	Portlaw, Waterford
Hogg, C. H. K.	S.C. & T.	Newark
Holmes, F.	Postman	Chesterfield
Hopkins, A.	Auxiliary Postman	Laceby, Grimsby
Hunter, A. T.	Postman	L.P.S., N.W. District
James, D.	Unestbd. Skilled Workman	Engrg. Dept., S.Wales District
Johnstone, A. J.	Sorter	L.P.S., Battersea District
Jones, E.	Auxiliary Postman	Guilsfield, Welshpool
Keefe, R.	Postman	Tullow, Carlow

The weekly bulletin of Post Office staff killed in the First World War – note the names of the Irish GPO staff.

(An Post archives)

Connaught Rangers officer Stephen Gwynn put it, is something that is common to several letters. Joseph Clarke, 'B' Company 2nd Battalion of the Fusiliers, wrote to Monica on 11 May 1916:

> I was sorry to hear of the rebel rising in Ireland … there is no one more sorry to hear of the rising than the Irish troops here, it worries them more than I can explain … Some of the men in this Battalion is [sic] very uneasy about the safety of their people, and one or two poor fellows have lost relatives in this scandalous affair … it is awfully hard to lose one's life out here, without being shot at home.[3]

Writing a day later, Christy Fox, who always signed his letters to Monica with a simple Christy, felt the same way. He lived close to the Linen Hall Barracks and, hearing about the intense fighting

3   Monica Roberts Collection RDFA/001/001 and following.

in the North King Street area, was particularly worried about his parents at home:

> … those Sinn Feiners are a lot of murderers they [*sic*] sooner Ireland gets rid of them they better they have brought a nice disgrace on the Old Country I can tell you they boys out here would like to catch a few of them and we would give them a rough time of it …

Some of the Fusiliers blamed the Germans for the rebellion, a response which was probably instinctive and Joseph Clarke's view was that:

> The Dublins would ask for nothing better than the rebels should be sent out here and have an encounter with some of their 'so called Allies' … no Irishmen will be sorry when they get justice meted out to them which in my opinion should be death by being shot.

Christy Fox, writing in another letter to Monica on 31 May, would also 'give them 2 oz. of lead', but then takes a more compassionate stance thinking of the Rising's participants as 'poor fools' who 'were dragged in to it by Connolly and a few more of his colleagues'. Remembering the 1913 strike, he adds that 'its they same click that brought on all that Distruction on our Dear Old Country [*sic*]'.

The effect of the Rising on the respect with which the Irish regiments in France were regarded by other troops is something which troubled Harry Loughlin. Writing to Monica on 17 June 1916, he says:

> I am very annoyed to think of the awful distruction done in our own City and don't in the least sympathise with the sentences passed upon the Sinn Feiners. I feel as my fellow countrymen feels [*sic*] disappointed and well sat upon by other Reg. who up to the affair would not say anything to us. And now we must suffer the loss of command in political matters.

The 'loss of command' that Private Loughlin felt was a practical manifestation of the changes that would quickly see Home Rule swept aside as passé and the old Irish Parliamentary Party destroyed. A man for whom it is hard not to feel a particular sympathy is Major William Redmond, MP, John Redmond's younger brother and the man whose personal example in joining the army in his fifties was influential in encouraging enlistment in Irish regiments. Some time before he was killed in June 1917, he wrote that 'in joining the Irish Brigade and going to France I sincerely believed, as all Irish soldiers do, that I was doing my best for the welfare of Ireland in every way'.[4]

In his evidence to the Hardinge Commission in 1916, Norway was asked to comment on the number of Post Office staff who had volunteered for the army. With the bulk of his official papers destroyed, he was cautious about giving precise figures, but he spoke with evident pride of the conduct of his staff noting that:

> Throughout the war many changes in the staff and the character of the work were rendered necessary, owing to the number of men who went on active service … Out of about 900 telegraphists or officials partially engaged in telegraphic work, nearly 50 per cent volunteered for active service.[5]

The Post Office's particular expertise in telegraphic and engineering work made it an obvious recruitment target during the war and the *Post Office Circular*, the weekly internal operational newsletter, testifies to the truth of Norway's statement in the names of Irish Post Office people which regularly appear amongst the long lists of staff killed or wounded in the war.

4   Quoted in *Major William Redmond*, Burns & Oates, p. 44.
5   *Royal Commission on the Rebellion in Ireland: Minutes of Evidence*, p. 63.

Ellie Kennedy, an auxiliary postwoman in Clonmel. Vacancies left by men who joined the army were often filled by women.

(An Post archives)

Prisoners of war were allowed to write one postcard a week. This one is from an Irish soldier imprisoned at Limburg, the camp where Roger Casement tried unsuccessfully to recruit Irishmen for the German army.

(An Post archives)

Conclusion

The story of the Post Office and its staff during the Rising is one that has lain in the shadows for close to a century now. Other circumstances and the future course of history meant that the actions and accounts of those who worked selflessly to maintain and restore Post Office services in the midst of the turmoil of Easter week were largely forgotten. The GPO, as a building, holds a special place in Irish history, but the men and women of the Post Office who did their duty – ordinary people caught up in extraordinary events – deserve to be remembered too. Norway's rather elegant tribute to them and his recommendation of a few days' extra holiday is characteristic of the man himself, at once sincere and yet restrained:

> It will never be fully known what the staff in Dublin faced during that bad week. The actual dangers were great: those reasonably apprehended were greater still, and it is not by any means certain that they are over even now. It is useless to attempt to appreciate degrees of merit in those who work steadily in such abnormal times, and it is better not to try. My staff as a whole did their work out of self-respect. But I think a little extra leave would be much appreciated.[1]

Those within Post Office ranks whose political views led them into disloyalty, and eventually rebellion, he would have regarded as misguided and their conduct wrong, but he was too honest a man not to respect men of principle when he came across them. He undoubtedly shouldered a heavy responsibility himself that week and acquitted himself well. He would return to a headquarters

---

1   BPMA Post 31/80B.

job in London in 1917 and retire in 1920, but for reasons both personal and public his time in Dublin's GPO could not have been easily forgotten.

Appendix 1

Warning letter issued to Post Office staff suspected of disloyalty

Sir,

The attention of the Postmaster-General has recently been called to the fact that you are a member of the Irish Volunteers under the leadership of a Committee presided over by Mr John McNeill. The Postmaster-General has also been apprised of the open hostility of this organisation to recruitment in the Forces of the Crown and, generally, to the Government under which you are serving. Of this, the public utterances of the leaders of the organisation and matter contained in the newspaper which purports to be its official organ are sufficient evidence.

While it appears to the Postmaster-General that an openly hostile attitude towards the Government, such as is indicated by membership of the body referred to, by taking part in its exercises and by association with its leaders in its business would at any time be improper in a member of the Civil Service, such an attitude in the time of war on the part of persons entrusted with business of the State is fraught with risk to the country which no Government is justified in incurring.

In these circumstances, I am directed to call on you to cease all connection with the Irish Volunteers or any other organisation pursuing similar objects, and to inform you that if you fail to comply with this direction the Postmaster-General will have no alternative but to dismiss you from your appointment in the Post Office without further warning.

The letter, submitted by A. H. Norway in evidence to the Hardinge Commission, was sent by the Postmaster General to the following Post Office staff:

C. Collins	Sorter	Accountant's Branch
P. O'Keeffe	Sorter	Accountant's Branch
J. McKenna	Sorter	Accountant's Branch
T. Dolan		Engineering Department
N. Cremen		Stores Department
T. Crowley	Sub-Postmaster	Ballylanders
W. Cavanagh	Rural Postman	Rathvilly
W. Regan	Rural Postman	Moycullen, Galway

APPENDIX 2

STAFF WHOSE CONDUCT DURING THE RISING MERITED SPECIAL MENTION

Mr Boyle	Sorting Clerk & Telegraphist – Telegraph Office
Coonan, J. J.	Principal Clerk – Secretary's Office
Doak, H.	Assistant Engineer – Engineering
Fogarty, J. J.	Sorting Clerk & Telegraphist – Telegraph Office
Galbally, L. W.	Sorting Clerk & Telegraphist – Telegraph Office
Gomersall, E.	Superintending Engineer – Engineering Branch
Miss Gordon	Assistant Supervisor – Telegraph Office
Guthrie, S. S.	Superintendent – Telegraph Office
Heaney, W. J.	Overseer – Kingsbridge Telegraph Office
Kenny, J. J.	Controller – Telegraph Office
Jones J.	Inspector – Engineering Branch
Mann, E. W.	Unestablished Porter – Stores Branch
Norway, A. H.	Secretary – GPO Dublin
Patchell, M.	Assistant Inspector of Postmen – DPD
Pemberton, W. A.	Assistant Superintendent – Telegraph Office
Reeves, J. H.	First Class Clerk – Stores Branch
Shaw, J. H.	Executive Engineer – Engineering Branch
Tipping, H. J.	Controller – Dublin Postal District
Winter, J.	Senior Inspector – Engineering Branch

While their names are not recorded, the bravery of the staff on duty in the Crown Alley Telephone Exchange is singled out as especially meritorious. The postmasters of Belfast, Cork and Kingstown are also thanked for the way in which they made special arrangements during the crisis.

Tipping's list, divided into its A, B and C classes of Dublin Postal District staff who ran various degrees of additional risk in the course of their duties during the Rising, runs to 129 names, mostly postmen, but includes also some telegraphists and sub-postmasters. Their duties involved mail preparation, security work, payment of allowances and sometimes just attendance at places like Ranelagh, Portobello and James's Street offices during periods of danger.

Local management in other Post Office departments, notably the telegraph and engineering sections, prepared lists of staff who were on duty during the insurrection and these people would have been able to avail of the extra 'rebellion leave' which Norway put in place to reward their service.

APPENDIX 3

STAFF SUSPECTED OF COMPLICITY

This list represents Post Office staff suspected of complicity in the Rising. With the exception of the two asterisked names which were added by Norway, Secretary of the Post Office, it was prepared for the Under Secretary, Dublin Castle, on the basis of special branch intelligence reports. The Wilson-Byrne commission examined the cases of civil servants on suspension at the time of their inquiry. They did not deal with those restored to duty before it began nor with those who still remained in military custody. Since the special branch list had been compiled before the Wilson-Byrne commission was set up, some suspects were no longer in military custody (MC) but remained under suspension and were duly examined by the committee.

Name	Grade	Branch/Office	Status	Wilson-Byrne
Richard J. Mulcahy	Clerk	Engineering	MC	
John O'Callaghan	CA	Engineering	MC	Dismiss
A. J. Fitzpatrick	CA	Engineering	MC	Dismiss
James J. Tyrell	CA	Engineering	MC	Dismiss
James Byrne	CA	Engineering	MC	Dismiss
John J. Twamley	CA	Engineering	MC	
Francis Byrne	CA	Engineering	MC	Dismiss
Martin King	CA	Engineering	MC	Dismiss
Francis Pollard	Youth	Engineering	MC	Dismiss

Joseph Lyons	Clerk (II)	GPO	MC	
Patrick O'Keeffe	Sorter Tracer	GPO	MC	
John Hayes	SC&T	GPO	MC	Dismiss
M. J. Collins	SC&T	GPO	MC	Dismiss
James F. Breslin	SC&T	Ferns	MC	Reinstate
Philip Murphy	Postman	Enniscorthy	MC	
Thomas Maher	Postman	Enniscorthy	MC	
M. Smith	Postman	Athgarvan, Newbridge	MC	
Christopher Caulfield	Postman	Athenry	MC	
Patrick Ryan	Postman	Cloughran, Dublin	MC	
Patrick O'Leary	Boy Messenger	Dublin	MC	
Daniel Buckley	Telephone Attendant	Maynooth	MC	
Dr Edward Dundon	Medical Attendant	Boris, Carlow	MC	
William Archer	SC&T	Dublin	S	Reinstate
Michael J. O'Neill	SC&T	Ferns	S	Reinstate
John O'Neill	SC&T	Enniscorthy	S	Reinstate
P. J. McDonnell	Clerk (II)	Dublin	S	Dismiss
John Darcy	Postman	Dublin	S	Reinstate
James M. Heery	CA	Dublin	S	Dismiss
James Haugh	SC&T	Waterford	S	
P. C. Mahony	SC&T	Dungarvan	S	
Michael McSweeney	Clerk	Waterford	S	
William Larkin	Postman	Waterford	S	Reinstate
Patrick Kehoe	Auxiliary Postman	Bridgetown, Wexford	S	Reinstate

John Murphy	Auxiliary Postman	Bridgetown, Wexford	S	Reinstate
John Stafford	Auxiliary Postman	Ballymitty, Wexford	S	Reinstate
D. M. de Loughry	SC&T	Kilkenny	S	Reinstate
F. McCarthy	SC&T	Kilkenny	S	Reinstate
Michael Cremen	Clerk (III)	Stores	R	
William S. O'Doherty	Assistant Clerk	Stores	R	
John McGinn	Postman	Rockcorry, Monaghan	R	
F. H. Clarke	Postman	Rockcorry, Monaghan	R	
Joseph Kenny	Postman	Rathangan, Kildare	R	
Patrick Kenny	Postman	Rathangan, Kildare	R	
Christopher Kenny	Postman	Rathangan, Kildare	R	
Pat Hughes*	Sorting Clerk	Dundalk	–	
J. Henigan*	Postman	Cork	–	Dismiss

Note: CA is Clerical Assistant and SC&T Sorting Clerk & Telegraphist. MC denotes in military custody, S under suspension and R restored to duty.

APPENDIX 4

A NOTE ON PRIMARY SOURCE MATERIAL

The destruction of both Post Office and Public Record Office papers in Dublin makes the British Postal Museum and Archive the most important source for information on the Irish Post Office prior to independence. The memoranda and official reports I have drawn on are to be found principally in files under the following headings.

Post 14/336
Post 31/36
Post 31/80
Post 31/80B
Post 31/91A
Post 56/177
Post 56/178
Post 56/179

To these must be added Norway's important memoir, *Irish Experiences in War*, a photocopy of which is with the Ó Broin papers in the National Library (MS 24,894). Keith Jeffery also made it available in *The Sinn Féin Rebellion as They Saw It* (Irish Academic Press 1999). He also was responsible for including the report of the Wilson-Byrne Inquiry, not previously published, in his very useful collection of 1916 documents, *The GPO and the Easter Rising* (Irish Academic Press 2005). The original, neatly initialled by Lord Wimborne, Lord Lieutenant, is in the United Kingdom National Archives at CO 904/25/1.

The National Library's O'Neill photograph album (Album 107) is in the National Photographic Archive. Prepared by J. W. O'Neill of the Post Office, similar material is also housed at the BPMA. An Post's archives contain some relevant printed material as well as occasional manuscript registers and establishment books that escaped destruction.

The United Kingdom's National Archives at Kew hold the Royal Irish Constabulary's special branch files, CO 904/196, amongst which are a few that concern Post Office staff who were the subject of particular investigation in the period leading up to the Rising.

The Department of Defence's Military Archives house the large collection of witness statements (BMH WS series) provided to the Bureau of Military History by people associated with the Rising and War of Independence. Again there is some relevant Post Office staff material here and it is illuminating to compare the surveillance reports of detectives in 1916 with the statements provided by the protagonists themselves a generation later.

Norway's Hardinge Commission evidence on 1916 is to be found in *The Royal Commission on the Rebellion in Ireland: Minutes of Evidence and Appendix of Documents* (Cd. 8311 1916). His wife's *The Sinn Fein Rebellion as I saw it* (London 1916) is full of Post Office interest and provides little personal touches that add colour and feeling to our understanding of the Rising.

The Monica Roberts Collection of First World War letters is part of the Royal Dublin Fusiliers Archive held within the Dublin City Archives at the Gilbert Library.

Many general histories as well as accounts and memoirs of the Rising have been helpful in providing additional information.

Bibliography

1916 Rebellion Handbook (first published by the *Weekly Irish Times*, The Mourne River Press reprint, 1998)

A Record of the Irish rebellion of 1916 (*Irish Life*, Dublin, 1916)

Bealey, F., *Post Office Engineering Union – History of the Post Office Engineers 1870–1970* (Bachman and Turner, London, 1976)

Bouch, J. J., *The Republican Proclamation of Easter Monday, 1916*, Publications of the Bibliographical Society of Ireland, Vol. V (Dublin, 1936)

Brennan-Whitmore W. J., *Dublin Burning – The Easter Rising from behind the Barricades* (Gill & Macmillan, Dublin, 1996)

Caulfield, M., *The Easter Rebellion* (Gill & Macmillan, Dublin, 1995)

Coogan, T. P., *1916: The Easter Rising* (Phoenix, London, 2001)

Craig, M., *Dublin 1660–1860* (Hodges Figgis, Dublin & Cresset Press London, 1952)

Cuimhneachán 1916, A Commemorative Exhibition of the Irish Rebellion 1916 (National Gallery of Ireland, Dublin, 1966)

De Paor, L., *On the Easter Proclamation and other Declarations* (Four Courts Press, Dublin, 1997)

Father Henry, O.F.M. Cap. (ed.), *The Capuchin Annual 1966* (Dublin, 1966)

Feldman, D., *Handbook of Irish Philately* (David Feldman Limited & The Dolmen Press Limited, Dublin, 1968)

Ferguson, S., *At the Heart of Events – Dublin's General Post Office* (An Post, Dublin, 2007)

Fitzgerald, D., *Desmond's Rising – Memoirs 1913 to Easter 1916* (Liberties Press, Dublin, 2006)

Fox, R.M., *The History of the Irish Citizen Army* (James Duffy & Co., Dublin, 1944)

French, R.B.D., 'J. O. Hannay', in *Hermathena – A Dublin University Review* No. CII (Dublin University Press, Dublin, 1966)

Gomersall, E. 'Irish Rebellion, 1916' in *The Post Office Electrical Engineers' Journal*, Vol. IX (London, 1916)

Gorham, M., *Forty Years of Irish Broadcasting* (The Talbot Press Limited, Dublin, 1967)

Hopkinson, M. (ed.), *Frank Henderson's Easter Rising* (Cork University Press, Cork, 1998)

Irish Independent (Dublin 1916)

Irwin, W., *Betrayal in Ireland* (The Northern Whig, Belfast, no date)

Jeffery, K. (ed.), *The Sinn Féin Rebellion as They Saw It* (Irish Academic Press, Dublin, 1999)

Jeffery, K., *The GPO and the Easter Rising* (Irish Academic Press, Dublin, 2006)

Kenny, M., *The Road to Freedom – Photographs and Memorabilia from the 1916 Rising and afterwards* (Country House, Dublin, 2001)

Lynch, D., *The IRB and the 1916 Rising* (Mercier Press, Cork, 1957)

Mac Lochlainn P. F. (ed.), *Last Words – Letters and Statements of the Leaders executed after the Rising at Easter 1916* (The Stationery Office, Dublin, 1990)

MacMahon, B., 'The Monica Roberts Collection of Letters from the Western Front, 1914–1918', in *The Irish Sword*, Vol. XXVI (Dublin, 2008–2009)

Mulcahy, R., *Richard Mulcahy (1886–1971): a family memoir* (Aurelian Press, Dublin, 1999)

Norway, A. H., *History of the Post-Office Packet Service between the Years 1793–1815* (Macmillan and Co., London, 1895)

Norway, A. H., 'Irish Experiences in War', in Jeffery, K. (ed.), *The Sinn Féin Rebellion as They Saw It* (Irish Academic Press, Dublin, 1999)

Norway, Mrs H., *The Sinn Fein Rebellion as I saw it* (Smith, Elder & Co., London, 1916)

Nowlan, K. B. (ed.), *The Making of 1916* (Stationery Office, Dublin, 1966)

Ó Broin, L., *Dublin Castle and the 1916 Rising* (Helicon Limited, Dublin, 1966)

O'Connor, J., *The 1916 Proclamation* (Anvil Books, Dublin, 1999)

O'Hegarty P. S., *The Victory of Sinn Féin* (University College Dublin Press, Dublin, 1998)

O'Neill, M., *From Parnell to De Valera – A biography of Jennie Wyse Power 1858–1941* (Blackwater Press, Dublin, 1991)

Oidhreacht 1916–1966 (Oifig an tSoláthair, Baile Átha Cliath)

Pratt, A. G. and Mogg, G., *Notes on Telegraphy* (Co-operative Printing Society Limited, London, 1910)

Purdon, E., *The 1916 Rising* (Mercier Press, Cork, 1999)

Redmond, W. H. K., *Trench Pictures from France* (Andrew Melrose Ltd, London, 1917)

Redmond, W. H. K., *Major William Redmond* (Burns & Oates, London, no date)

Reports of the Postmaster General on the Post Office (HMSO, London)

Ryan, A., *Witnesses – Inside the Easter Rising* (Liberties Press, Dublin, 2005)

Shute, N., *Slide Rule – Autobiography of an Engineer* (Heinemann, London, 1954)

Sinn Féin Weekly (Dublin, 1908)

St. Martin's-Le-Grand (London)

The Irish Builder, 1916 (Dublin)

The Irish Postal and Telegraph Guardian 1916 (Dublin)

The Post Office Dublin Directory and Calendar 1916 (Alex Thom, Dublin)

The Royal Commission on the Rebellion in Ireland – Minutes of Evidence and Appendix of Documents (HMSO, London, 1916)

Walsh J. J., *Recollections of a Rebel* (The Kerryman Ltd., Tralee, 1944)

Warwick-Haller, A. & S. (eds), *Letters from Dublin, Easter 1916 – Alfred Fannin's Diary of the Rising* (Irish Academic Press, Dublin, 1995)